CARP
THE ME...

**A step-by-step guide to understanding and constructing
the tried-and-tested rigs used by expert carp anglers**

COMPILED BY STEVE BROAD

Second Edition 2015

British Library Cataloguing in Publication Data

Carp Rigs The Mechanics
Carp Angling
Angling Publications Ltd.

ISBN: 978-1-871700-88-6

Compiled by Steve Broad of Angling Publications Ltd.
Designed by Gary Hood of Angling Publications Ltd.
Illustrations by Andy Steer and Mr & Mrs Smith

CARP RIGS: THE MECHANICS
CONTENTS

INTRODUCTION
BY STEVE BROAD

Choosing the right rig for the situation you are facing is never easy, simply because you have to take so many variables into consideration. Experienced anglers have knowledge going back over many years to fall back on, which helps them make the right decision. We've called upon this vast pool of knowledge to create this rig book and give you all the information you need to make the right rig choice every single time.

It is also important to keep up to date with the very latest rig components and materials. Tackle manufacture is forever evolving and creating everything

The mega-popular Chod Rig that was made famous by Terry Hearn, led to the capture of the 44lb+ common pictured above.

from super-sharp hooks to thinner but stronger reel lines, and advancements are happening

on an almost daily basis. Often these new products make rig construction easier, more efficient, and harder wearing. The result of this is that we as anglers have access to all the bits and pieces we need to make the best possible presentation.

This book contains everything you will ever need to know about rigs, and is aimed at every carp angler, regardless of age or experience. Carp fishing is a forever evolving thing, so you need the very latest information to stay one step ahead of the crowd. There are no certainties in our sport, but what we are aiming to do is give you the facts that will steer you in the right direction when it comes to rig choice.

We have covered what is available, right from the line on the reel to the very last bit of the rig, the hook, to help you make an informed decision about the fundamentals of your setup. You will need to know a few easy-to-master knots, and be able to choose the right lead for the job. Lead systems are explained, and we reveal the best rigs, whether you want to use a pop-up, bottom bait, or critically-balanced presentation.

Also included are nine great guest chapters that highlight the favourite rigs of the following top-class anglers: Terry Hearn, Frank Warwick, Tim Paisley, Terry Dempsey, Rob Nunn, Lewis Read, Nick Burrage, Mark Pitchers, and Ken South. We'd like to thank these people for their extensive input into this book.

One final thing; you should always remember that it doesn't matter how good your rig is if you put it in the wrong place, so always think of the bigger picture.

Many people can't be bothered with the hassle of tying a solid bag, but the effort is worthwhile and is a technique that should be mastered.

A seldom-caught mirror that succumbed to a solid PVA bag presentation, cast into very thick weed.

CHAPTER 1
REEL LINES
THE MAJOR CONNECTION

Any fishing line we use is the major connection between us and the fish we are trying to catch, so it needs to have a number of characteristics that allow us to use it: thinness, strength, abrasion-resistance, suppleness, ability to be knotted, and cost, are all factors which come into play. So, as you can see, there are plenty of criteria to be met before we even arrive at the right line for the specialist situations we face. There is something else you need to consider when buying line for your reel, and that is – what does it actually break at? The fishing industry is only just starting to regulate itself when it comes to standardisation of line so we are still in a situation where a line labelled 12lb breaking strain can actually break at anywhere between 10 and 20lb depending on the manufacturer. The breaking strains of most lines which are in use at the moment are underrated, so you may find a claimed 8lb line actually breaks at 14lb. We recommend that you consider diameter and breaking strain to assess which line is best for the job in hand, and that's why we have reproduced the line chart at the end of this chapter, with kind permission from the guys at The Tackle Box. There is also another curve ball in the line equation, and that's the use of braid. Most UK anglers only really use it for spod and marker work, but there are some pioneers out there who swear by it as a reel line, as we'll explain later in this chapter.

NYLON

The correct name for nylon is actually monofilament; this describes how it is manufactured, which is by extruding a single strand of polymer. This type of line was introduced about 70 years ago and soon gained favour because it was cheap and easy to make, but still had the important properties that made it useful for anglers. It also had an inherent stretch which many anglers found useful when playing big fish and reacting to any sudden lunges.

To decide which line is best for you, it is wise to consider where and how the vast majority of your fishing is undertaken. If the venue that you are tackling is packed with weed or snags then you need a robust, strong line that is up to the harshness of the environment. We would recommend a line with a high diameter of around 0.38mm or higher, which will probably break at over 20lb, and will offer plenty of abrasion-resistance. The downside of using this line is its thickness and wiry nature, which will reduce your ability to cast. For most standard fishing situations, a line of roughly 0.33mm diameter will be ideal. It will break at around 12lb or above and will be sufficiently user-friendly to allow you to cast reasonable distances. A line of that breaking strain is strong

enough for most of the open-water fishing in this country, but if you travel abroad then you may have to consider using a stronger line.

To complicate matters further, we now have a host of new lines to consider, and these are copolymers, which at first glance appear to be the same as nylon. In fact, rather than being produced from a single polymer they are derived from a mixture, which tends to give them improved characteristics. They are often thinner, very abrasion-resistant for the diameter, have controlled stretch, and have excellent knot strength. On the downside, they are still slightly more expensive than standard nylon lines.

FLUOROCARBON

If you listen to the hype, fluorocarbon reel lines are the must-have accessory, but like anything else there are pros and cons to consider when using them. From a fishing point of view, this product has two main advantages. Firstly, it is very hard to see, thanks to the fact that it has a refractive light index very similar to water. Secondly, it sinks like a brick, making it useful for anglers because they can allow their lines to lie on the lakebed out of the way of moving fish.

This type of reel line also has a number of other plus points in its favour, in that it doesn't deteriorate as quickly as mono, is less affected by the sun, and has a lot less stretch than nylon.

On the downside, fluorocarbon is expensive, and isn't as easy to use as standard lines. It is very difficult to knot to its full potential, and choice of knot and ensuring that it is properly lubricated is essential. Its weight, diameter, and wiry nature also mean that it is not a brilliant casting line and many anglers don't use it for this reason alone. The reality is that it does have a valid place in carp fishing, but there is a time and a place to use it to the best advantage.

BRAID

Make no mistake, braid is a huge asset when it comes to fishing, but making the right choice is essential. For ease we will split braid into two categories, sinking and floating, and reveal the situations that each variety is best suited for.

Most floating braids are exceptionally thin, making them excellent casting lines, and in the right hands immense distances can be achieved. This makes it perfect for very specialist long-range fishing techniques, but there are guidelines that must be followed. It is difficult to spool up correctly and needs to be wet and loaded onto the reel under pressure. In addition you also need to slightly under-fill your spools. Both of these things help to minimise the bane of the braid user's life – wind knots. These occur when the thin, light braid comes off the spool too quickly and forms a huge bird's nest which is often impossible to untangle. Loading it correctly and always wetting the braid before use will keep these frustrating occurrences to an absolute minimum.

Most anglers use these types of braid for spod and marker work because they cast

well. The fact that braids float aids line pickup when reeling in a spod, which allows you to skip it across the surface for an easy retrieve. The lack of stretch also makes it perfect for marker work, and the feel of the nature of the lakebed is transmitted back up the line and helps the angler form a mental image of what is below the surface.

Anglers who fish large waters and boat their baits out huge distances also often rely on braid. With its low diameter for its breaking strain, more can be fitted on a reel spool. The lack of stretch also means better bite indication, something

that is a must when fishing over 200m where a fish can move the rig several metres without anything happening at the rod end. The no-stretch qualities of braid make it the first choice for many anglers when they are fishing snag situations, where the stretch in nylon would allow a taking fish to find the sanctuary of the snags.

Sinking braid does exactly what it says on the box, and in most cases sinks because it has fibres woven into it that absorb water, making it heavy. This type of braid is often thicker than standard braid and, once wet, tends to cast relatively poorly. But to many anglers, the lack of stretch, sinking properties, low deterioration rate and strength make it a worthwhile proposition as a reel line

Make of Line	Stated Strain	Average Strain	Stated Diameter	Measured Diameter
NYLON				
Berkley Big Game Green	10lb	13.88lb	0.31mm	0.30mm
	12lb	15.75lb	0.36mm	0.34mm
	15lb	20.75lb	0.38mm	0.38mm
Daiwa Sensor Brown	4lb	5.88lb	0.205mm	0.20mm
	6lb	8.5lb	0.235mm	0.22mm
	8lb	10.75lb	0.26mm	0.25mm
	10lb	14.63lb	0.31mm	0.30mm
	12lb	16.5lb	0.33mm	0.32mm
	15lb	17.63lb	0.37mm	0.36mm
	18lb	21.63lb	0.405mm	0.40mm
	20lb	25lb	0.435mm	0.43mm
	25lb	31lb	0.520mm	0.51mm
	30lb	32.13lb	0.570mm	0.57mm
Daiwa Sensor Clear	8lb	10.12lb	0.26mm	0.25mm
	10lb	15.87lb	0.31mm	0.30mm
	12lb	16.75lb	0.33mm	0.32mm
	15lb	21.37lb	0.37mm	0.35mm
	18lb	24.75lb	0.405mm	0.40mm
E•S•P Crystal Carp Mono	10lb	11.13lb	0.30mm	0.31mm
	12lb	13.38lb	0.325mm	0.32mm
	15lb	15lb	0.35mm	0.36mm
	18lb	17.63lb	0.375mm	0.375mm
E•S•P Olive Carp Mono	10lb	11.0lb	0.30mm	0.28mm
	12lb	12.63lb	0.325mm	0.30mm
	15lb	14.13lb	0.35mm	0.32mm
	18lb	16.5lb	0.375mm	0.35mm
E•S•P Syncro XT	10lb	14lb	0.30mm	0.29mm
	12lb	15.75lb	0.33mm	0.31mm
	15lb	21.75lb	0.37mm	0.35mm
	18lb	21.63lb	0.40mm	0.39mm
Fox Exocet Green	13lb	14.67lb	0.309mm	0.29mm
	16lb	14.22lb	0.331mm	0.32mm
	18lb	16.36lb	0.35mm	0.33mm
Fox Soft Steel Camo	10lb	13.5lb	0.286mm	0.28mm
	12lb	13.63lb	0.309mm	0.31mm
	15lb	15lb	0.331mm	0.33mm
Gardner GR60	12lb	18.75lb	0.35mm	0.35mm
	15lb	24lb	0.40mm	0.40mm
Gardner GR60X Clear	12lb	15.88lb	0.35mm	0.34mm
	15lb	17.5lb	0.40mm	0.38mm
Gardner GR60X Green	12lb	16lb	0.35mm	0.32mm
	15lb	18.88lb	0.40mm	0.39mm
Gold Label Pro Clear	10lb	12.13lb	0.26mm	0.26mm
	12lb	14.5lb	0.29mm	0.29mm
	16lb	19.75lb	0.34mm	0.34mm
	20lb	24.75lb	0.40mm	0.38mm
Gold Label Pro Gold	8lb	11.38lb	0.28mm	0.27mm
	10lb	11.88lb	0.305mm	0.29mm
	12lb	17.5lb	0.355mm	0.35mm
	15lb	22lb	0.38mm	0.38mm
Gold Label Pro Distance	10lb	15.13lb	0.30mm	0.29mm
	12lb	18.75lb	0.35mm	0.34mm
	15lb	17.63lb	0.38mm	0.38mm
Korda Adrena-Line	10lb	11.75lb	0.30mm	0.30mm
	12lb	13.25lb	0.33mm	0.33mm
	15lb	15.63lb	0.35mm	0.36mm
	18lb	17.63lb	0.38mm	0.39mm
Korda Kruiser Control	6lb	9.38lb	0.25mm	0.24mm
	8lb	11.75lb	0.28mm	0.28mm
	10lb	11.25lb	0.30mm	0.29mm
	12lb	16.25lb	0.33mm	0.33mm
Korda Subline Brown	10lb	13.5lb	0.30mm	0.30mm
	12lb	17.13lb	0.35mm	0.36mm
	15lb	19.25lb	0.40mm	0.40mm
	20lb	22.00lb	0.43mm	0.43mm
Korda Subline Green	10lb	12.88lb	0.30mm	0.29mm
	12lb	17.88lb	0.35mm	0.35mm
	15lb	18.88lb	0.40mm	0.39mm
	20lb	22.38lb	0.43mm	0.42mm
Krystonite	8lb	8.62lb	0.25mm	0.24mm
	10lb	13.62lb	0.29mm	0.28mm
	12lb	13.75lb	0.31mm	0.30mm
	15lb	16.12lb	0.36mm	0.35mm
	18lb	22.5lb	0.41mm	0.40mm
Nash NXT D-Cam Mono	12lb	18.38lb	0.35mm	0.34mm
	15lb	21.25lb	0.38mm	0.39mm
	18lb	24.88lb	0.43mm	0.43mm
Shimano Catana	8lb	14.13lb	0.28mm	0.28mm
	10lb	16lb	0.30mm	0.30mm
	12lb	18.88lb	0.33mm	0.33mm
	15lb	20.5lb	0.35mm	0.35mm
Shimano Tribal Carp	10lb	13.41lb	0.305mm	0.26mm
	12lb	15.72lb	0.33mm	0.32mm
	15lb	19.52lb	0.38mm	0.39mm
TF Gear Nan-Tec Mono Red Mist	12lb	13.41lb	0.30mm	0.27mm
	15lb	16.62lb	0.35mm	0.34mm

Make of Line	Stated Strain	Average Strain	Stated Diameter	Measured Diameter
NYLON				
Ultima Power Carp Clear	10lb	14.38lb	0.28mm	0.29mm
	12lb	17.50lb	0.31mm	0.31mm
	14lb	19.63lb	0.33mm	0.34mm
	16lb	22lb	0.36mm	0.38mm
	18lb	27.25lb	0.38mm	0.42mm
Ultima Power Carp Ultra	12lb	14.38lb	0.31mm	0.31mm
	14lb	9lb	0.33mm	0.33mm
	16lb	10.88lb	0.36mm	0.38mm
	18lb	13.63lb	0.38mm	??????
Ultima Power Carp XR	12lb	14.38lb	0.31mm	0.31mm
	14lb	17.13lb	0.34mm	0.35mm
	16lb	17.0lb	0.36mm	0.37mm
	18lb	17.63lb	0.38mm	0.40mm
FLUOROCARBON				
Berkley Super Strong 100% Fluorocarbon	12lb	13lb	0.33mm	0.33mm
	15lb	14.5lb	0.365mm	0.365mm
	17lb	14.89lb	Unstated	0.38mm
Daiwa Floorit Brown	10lb	9.26lb	0.27mm	0.26mm
	12lb	10.55lb	0.31mm	0.28mm
	14lb	14.13lb	0.33mm	0.34mm
	17lb	16.08lb	0.37mm	0.38mm
Daiwa Floorit Clear	12lb	11.09lb	0.31mm	0.28mm
	14lb	13.14lb	0.33mm	0.34mm
	17lb	16.08lb	0.37mm	0.38mm
Fox Illusion® XS	12lb	7.88lb	0.30mm	0.27mm
	15lb	10.25lb	0.35mm	0.34mm
	18lb	13.5lb	0.38mm	0.38mm
Gardner Mirage	12lb	11.75lb	0.33mm	0.33mm
	14lb	12.88lb	0.35mm	0.35mm
	16lb	13.38lb	0.37mm	0.36mm
Korda Kontour	12lb	11.5lb	0.33mm	0.31mm
TF Gear Secret Trap	17lb	13.38lb	0.35mm	0.35mm
Ultima Pure Power Fluorocarbon Clear	12lb	9.38lb	0.30mm	0.30mm
	14lb	10.75lb	0.32mm	0.32mm
	16lb	11.5lb	0.35mm	0.35mm
Ultima Pure Power Fluorocarbon Green	12lb	8.25lb	0.30mm	0.30mm
	14lb	10.5lb	0.32mm	0.32mm
	16lb	13.0lb	0.35mm	0.35mm
X Line	12lb	9.38lb	0.26mm	0.28mm
	15lb	10.25lb	0.31mm	0.29mm
	17lb	11.13lb	0.33mm	0.31mm
	20lb	12.63lb	0.37mm	0.35mm
X2 Secure	15lb	13.82lb	0.30mm	0.31mm
	20lb	15.14lb	0.35mm	0.34mm
BRAID				
Berkley Fireline Braid	14lb	21.38lb	0.23mm	0.28mm
	20lb	26.38lb	0.30mm	0.34mm
	30lb	38.13lb	0.36mm	0.43mm
Berkley Fireline Tournament Exceed	14lb	21lb	0.23mm	0.26mm
	20lb	24.88lb	0.30mm	0.33mm
	30lb	38.13lb	0.36mm	0.43mm
Berkley Nanofil	12.64kg (28lb)	12lb	0.20mm	0.23mm
Berkley Whiplash Braid	30lb	15.88lb	0.06mm	0.20mm
	30lb	17.63lb	0.10mm	0.26mm
Daiwa Tournament 8 Braid	50lb	26lb	0.26mm	0.26mm
Dynon SK Braid	22lb	19.88lb	Unstated	0.30mm
	34lb	27.25lb	Unstated	0.39mm
E•S•P Spod & Marker Braid	20lb	18.88lb	0.30mm	0.38mm
Fox Exocet Distance Spod & Marker Braid	23lb	13.5lb	0.18mm	0.24mm
Fox Gravitron Pro	15lb	13.88lb	0.30mm	0.31mm
	20lb	18.13lb	0.35mm	0.37mm
	25lb	21.37lb	0.40mm	0.38mm
Nash Bullet Braid	15lb	19.5lb	0.30mm	0.32mm
	20lb	20.63lb	0.35mm	0.34mm
	25lb	22.63lb	0.40mm	0.34mm
Nash NXT Bullet Braid	15lb	18.13lb	0.23mm	0.30mm
	20lb	23.63lb	0.30mm	0.35mm
	25lb	26.63lb	0.34mm	0.38mm
Spiderwire Ultracast Fluoro Braid	20lb	19lb	0.25mm	0.30mm
	30lb	23.63lb	0.30mm	0.31mm
TF Gear Banana Braid	30lb	24lb	0.28mm	0.24mm
Ultima Vertibraid	20lb	20.0lb	Unstated	0.25mm
	30lb	27.75lb	Unstated	0.34mm
X2 Durabraid	31.5lb (14.3kg)	21lb	0.20mm	0.24mm
	37lb (16.8kg)	24lb	0.25mm	0.32mm
	42lb (19.3kg)	27lb	0.30mm	0.34mm

REEL LINES

15

CHAPTER 2
BEHIND THE LEAD
LEADERS OF THE NEW SCHOOL

Take a look at any modern carp presentation and you will see it has a distinctive item of tackle between the hooklink and the reel line, whether this is tubing, leadcore, or some other form of leader. All of these items serve as different ways of achieving the same set of goals, namely camouflage, stopping tangles, and protection. Camouflage is the angler's attempt to fool the carp into believing that there is nothing untoward in the vicinity of the hookbait. This is achieved by pinning the line to the lakebed to make it as unobtrusive as possible, and matching the colour so that whatever you are using blends in with the bottom. Tangles occur because the hooklink wraps around the reel line as it flies through the air. The risk of

> All these items serve as different ways of achieving the same set of goals, namely camouflage, stopping tangles, and protection

this can be minimised by adding a stiffer and thicker section of tackle behind the lead. Finally, protection – this comes in two forms, the first of which is the protection of the reel line. Any form of leader or tubing helps to protect the line in the vicinity of the lead from abrasion, either from the lakebed or during the playing of a fish when the line can come into contact with an underwater obstacle. Then there is the protection of the fish itself, helping to reduce any rubbing along its flanks that could inadvertently occur during the fight. The range of products that can be used behind the lead is extensive and, as with everything else, is constantly evolving, but some old favourites still exist simply because they are so effective.

RIG TUBE

This is the original form of material that appeared behind the lead, and was really put into use for its anti-tangle properties in an era when braided hooklinks were the norm. Tubing has been in use for at least 30 years and in that time has changed markedly. Every rig-component manufacturer has a number of different tubing products all now specifically designed to cover a wide variety of different angling situations. Tubing comes in a range of diameters to deal with different lines, and a whole host of colours to suit your every need. More importantly, however, is the fact that all modern forms of tubing possess much improved properties: they sink, are very supple which allows them to sit better, and, once sitting on the lakebed, they remain straight rather than

curling up on themselves. A number of companies have also introduced tungsten-impregnated tubing which is very dense and often has a pleasant feel to it. This material really does take things to the next level and hugs the contours of the bottom. When it comes to actually using tubing, most modern varieties are very user-friendly. We would suggest that you use a piece that is always longer than your hooklink, and would go one step further by saying 60 to 90cm will achieve the best results in most situations. Most brands are easy to thread, but should you have any problems, a pole threader bought

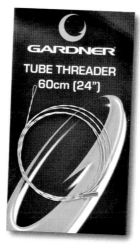

from your local tackle shop will make it easier. Lastly, always have one end of the tubing cut at an angle; this helps when fitting it into things like tail rubbers.

↑ Most modern forms of rig tubing are surprisingly supple, and will follow the contours of the lakebed.

↑ Cutting your rig tubing at an angle will help when connecting to other terminal tackle items such as tail rubbers.

BEHIND THE LEAD

18

LEADCORE

For use behind the lead, this material has become probably the number-one choice for many anglers, although its use is one that has divided the modern angling world, with many believing that it can be a dangerous product. The truth is that any form of leader used behind the lead which is stronger than the hooklink can be dangerous to carp, and could, in the worst case scenario, lead to a fish being tethered and perhaps, in an extreme case, harming itself. As with any product, plenty of thought should be given to all aspects of using leadcore for the safety of the fish, and even other anglers.

There is a vast array of different leadcore products that all have the same basic properties: a woven braid outer with a soft single strand of lead running through the centre. It can be knotted or spliced to make your own unique leaders. With practice, splicing can be mastered and means that leaders can be created easily and customised to suit very specific needs. If you can't get the hang of splicing – and don't worry, many can't – then there are pre-tied versions available. All manufacturers include comprehensive details on their packaging of how to use leadcore, and this includes everything from splicing to rigs.

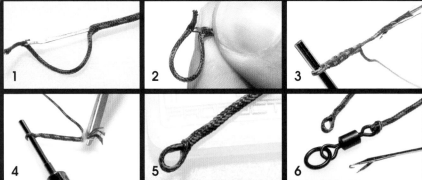

HOW TO SPLICE A LEADCORE LEADER

Firstly, remove around 8cm of the inner wire from a length of leadcore, before pushing a splicing needle through the centre of the leader, exiting after 2.5cm (1). Trap the tag end of the leader with the latched needle (2) and gently tease it back through the centre of the leadcore, using a tension bar to form the loop (3). Once you have pulled the tag end all the way through, carefully pull tight and trim the tag end (4) so that you are left with a neat loop like this (5). To attach a swivel, pass the leader through the eye, pass the other end of the leader through the loop and pull tight (6).

OTHER LEADERS

The carp world has moved on apace and there is a vast array of leaders made from a range of other materials, the most common of which is best described as a polyleader. It is generally a length of mono with a swivel attached at one end and a loop at the other, which is then encased in a polymer. This creates a very easy to use leader available from the likes of Korda, Nash and TF Gear. These products come in a variety of forms, depending on which manufacturer you choose, and are available in a range of colours.

A relatively new kid on the block is a product which is very similar to leadcore in every way, apart from one distinct fact: it doesn't have the lead in the centre. So it is still a hollow braid that is very dense and sinks, and can also be spliced or knotted, but it has the added advantage that it is super-supple. Several manufacturers have versions, including Solar, Taska and Fox.

There are also a couple of ways of hiding the line that don't fit in with the leader or tubing ethos. Some anglers want to keep the line pinned down but don't want to use any form of leader, and this can be achieved in a couple of different ways. You can either mould small blobs of tungsten putty up your reel line every few centimetres, or use a new little rig accessory called a Sinker. This is like a tungsten-impregnated float stop which can be threaded up the line to help sink it.

Revealed. The next generation of Korda leads.

Developed in response to popular demand, the textured finish becomes absorbed into its surroundings and practically disappears against most lake beds. The characteristics that allow the leads to take on sediment will also enable them to effectively take on flavours, glugs or dips, adding extra attraction around your rig.

For more information, klick www.korda.co.uk

CHAPTER 3
A WEIGHTY ISSUE
LEADS AND THEIR USES

Many people see a lead as just a casting aid, providing enough weight to simply position the rig in the desired spot, but in reality it is so much more. Yes, the lead is a tool to cast with, but it is also a method of anchoring your rig to your chosen spot, and finally it is a way of hooking fish when they pick up your rig. In this chapter, we'll discuss what lead styles are available and what they are best suited to.

It is important to understand that the actual weight of the lead is an important aspect of lead design. The heavier the lead, the more likely it is that the hook will penetrate properly when the carp moves with the hookbait. On the other hand, over a period of time, suspicious carp can become conditioned to 'feeling' for heavy leads, at which stage a very light lead may be more effective. Getting the weight of the lead right is all part of the fascination of the design of effective rigs.

ZIPP OR DISTANCE LEAD

This long, thin, elongated style of lead has been around for ages, and has basically remained the same for many years. It is the first choice of many anglers when it comes to casting long distances and works exceptionally well in a variety of different situations. The sleek extended design means it cuts through the air with ease and also flies very straight, which helps to keep tangles to a minimum and assists with gaining those extra yards.

Extended design to cut efficiently through the air to achieve maximum distance.

WEIGHT-FORWARD LEADS

There are loads of names and slightly varying designs for this style of lead, but they all follow the same basic principles. A long elongated tail with a bulbous weight-forward nose which helps it to fly very straight, the shape has been slightly tweaked by many companies. These leads cast just as well as the more streamlined Zipp-style but with the added benefit of having a large surface area when you are trying to feel the lead down at extreme range.

Weight-forward nose aids accuracy at range.

FLAT PEAR

This shape has almost become the standard lead for many anglers thanks to its versatility in every situation, apart from distance casting. Regardless of which company you buy this lead from it will be almost exactly the same design, proving just how good it is. The short, squat body with two flat sides serves two purposes; firstly, it is a great lead for bolt or self-hooking rigs, and secondly, it holds in place very well, perfect for staying where it lands when casting to small features like a gravel bar or island margin. Never underestimate this compact style of lead, because it will put more fish on the bank when used in the right place, and don't be afraid to use it in big sizes such as 5oz, which will make it very hard for a carp to deal with your rig.

Flat sides help the weight to stay in position on marginal slopes.

PEAR LEADS

In profile, very similar to the flat pear except that it has a rounded rather than a flat body. Again, this is a squat, compact design that casts very well and enhances the bolt effect of most rigs. This lead also comes in handy when fishing over areas of soft lakebed because it digs in, which increases the bolt effect of your rig. This shape is also very good for 'leading around' to feel the lakebed, and transmits a great deal of information back to the angler, and for many, this is reason enough to use this handy lead.

Great for 'reading' the lakebed.

GRIPPER LEADS

This style of lead has gained favour with many European anglers because it suits their style of fishing. Their rigs are often boated out long distances and are left in place for several days, and this shape helps to keep the rig firmly anchored in place. You will find these leads in anything from an ounce to nearly a pound in weight. However, don't think that they are just for this style of fishing; for short-range work they cast relatively well and will grip the lakebed. With the increase of river carping, many anglers prefer this type of lead because it holds station better in flowing water.

Knobbly surface grips the lakebed, keeping the rig in position, even in flowing water.

SQUARE LEADS

The thinking behind this design was to make a lead as dense as possible with a view to increasing its hooking potential, so improving on the more efficient ball-style. Ball leads obviously had a tendency to roll, so by flattening the side slightly the more user-friendly square lead was born. These leads aren't perfect in flight but you can still achieve good distances, and they are ideal when fishing for wary carp that have seen everything.

Compact shape aids self-hooking.

IN-LINE LEADS

Having the line running through the centre of the lead means the fish feels the full weight of the lead much quicker.

At one time, in the early years of carping, this style of lead was what most people used, but they slowly fell from favour. It was initially used so widely because of its great anti-tangle properties, but anglers soon realised that its nose-heavy design had some plus as well as some minus points. It is tangle-free, and is a great hooker because once the hooklink is straightened the fish automatically feels the full force of the lead. On the downside, the fact that the nose is heavy could affect how your rig sits in weed or silt. These leads are coming back into fashion because anglers now understand that they can be used over areas of firm lakebed to great effect. All the lead styles already discussed are available in in-line versions and many of their performance characteristics carry over. In-lines have also become very popular in specific styles of fishing such as PVA techniques and stalking, but more of that later.

SPECIALITY WEIGHTS

Please note the lack of the word lead here, as many of these products perform the same function but are made from different materials. The first and most obvious type is the Stonze range, in that they are exactly what it says on the box, a stone. The advantages of these is they are a natural product so they shouldn't harm the environment, and they also blend in very well over some types of bottom. You can also get a whole host of weights in the same patterns that we have discussed but which are made from different materials, like tungsten. Here are another couple of alternative lead types you might come across: Firstly there are marker leads, which have raised bumps on them to help you get a better feel of the features of the lakebed. Then there are Method leads designed to allow you to mould paste or groundbait around them. Finally, there is a very clever design of lead called the Trilobe or Elevator, which has a unique shape that sinks more slowly and also helps it rise quickly in the water on the retrieve, missing snags or bottom debris; a very popular style with some specialist anglers.

CHAPTER 4
LEAD SYSTEMS
CHOOSING THE RIGHT SETUP

How you attach your lead and how it performs underwater will have a bearing on your results, so you will have to choose the best setup for the situation you are faced with. The alternative lead setups include running leads, lead-on-the-end-of-the-line setups, fixed leads and semi-fixed leads. The choice of setup and the method of rig attachment will be mainly affected by the terrain you are fishing over, and that word 'lakebed' comes back into the equation.

LEAD CLIPS

This style of lead attachment has grown in popularity and is probably the most commonly used. Unfortunately it can also be the most misused, with anglers having little understanding of what they are trying to achieve. It is not always the best presentation but with a little thought and effort it is very effective, and worth mastering. The lead clip is designed to allow you to add a lead of your choice to the setup with ease, enabling you to cast well and be fairly tangle-free, and to be safe. If your clip is set correctly it should perform in a couple of different ways. It can either release the lead on the pickup so that the carp will immediately rise in the water,

eliminating the risk of the lead snagging in weedy or snaggy conditions. Or the lead can remain on the clip and only get dislodged should the fish encounter an underwater obstacle such as weed or branches, when it will be released.

The mechanics of the lead clip mean that is very effective in a wide variety of situations, including shallow silt, light weed, and areas of hard bottom. There are a number of varying styles of lead clip available; the only thing we would advise is that you understand how they work. When creating a system please try to stick with products from the same manufacturer because they are often designed to work together and complement each other.

↑ Some clips feature a pin which locks the swivel into place inside the barrel of the clip, resulting in the lead being dropped every time.

↑ You can also only just push the tail rubber in place, which allows the lead to fall off on the take.

RUNNING RIGS

Free-running rigs are simply when your lead slides on the line, rather than being fixed safely in place on your rig to create the bolt effect. This serves a couple of functions: the first is increased bite detection because your line pulls through your lead on the pickup, moving your line, and ultimately your bobbin, to give you a visible indication. Carp which are very rig-aware can also use the weight of a safely fixed lead to throw the hook, whereas with a running rig they have nothing to shake their heads against and thus jolt the hook out.

This type of presentation can be achieved in a variety of ways, from simply threading a swivel lead onto your reel line, adding a couple of beads between the lead and the hooklink swivel, then tying on your hooklink. There are also more specialised systems designed to achieve the same effect, or you can adapt a rig you already use. Lead clips and in-line leads can also be used free-running just by making some easy changes. Most lead clips work by trapping and fixing your hooklink swivel in place, meaning that the full force of the take is transferred to the lead, which ultimately comes off. Instead, you can replace the swivel with a clip that can still pull into the barrel of your lead clip, but not lock it in place to get a running presentation. The same is true of in-line leads when you remove the inner sleeve and use a buffer-style bead to stop the lead against the hooklink swivel; both very effective.

This arrangement from Solar converts a lead clip from being semi-fixed to running in one easy step.

This clearly shows how the new Fox in-line drop-off system works. This is perfect for solid bag fishing.

IN-LINE DROP-OFF PRESENTATIONS

In-line leads are proving very popular again following the introduction of a technique of allowing an in-line lead to safely come off the line on the take. This system is now widely used in a range of different fishing setups like Zig fishing and solid PVA bag work. We even know of anglers who use it in conjunction with very heavy in-line leads when creating sneakily prepared margin traps, and lowering

their presentation carefully into position. This rig usually relies on some form of leader, but not always, and specialised leads can also be used by the angler if they deem it necessary.

Our preferred technique is to use a short leader of any material on which you have a loop at one end and a ring swivel that is attached to the leader via the ring. You'll also need a tail rubber in place. You then push the swivel into the nose of the in-line, then run the leader around the body

of the lead before trapping it in place over the insert with the tail rubber. With the hooklink attached to the ring on the swivel, when a carp picks up the bait and bolts, the force pulls the swivel free and allows the lead to drop free.

This way of setting up this presentation is a little rough-and-ready and companies like Fox produce some very neat and clever rig accessories that make creating the perfect drop-off in-line presentation very simple. It is definitely a setup worth mastering.

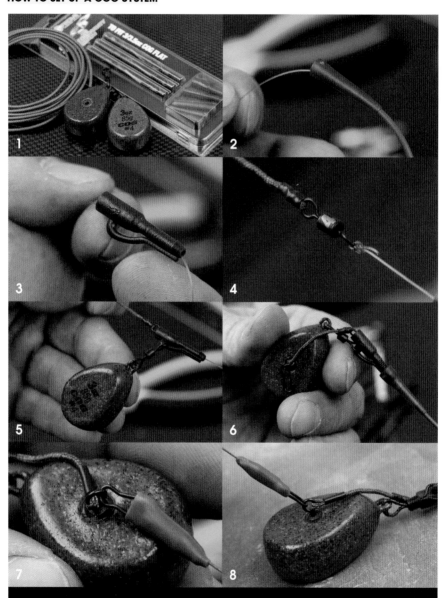

(1) Here are all the components you need to set up this system. (2) Thread a tail rubber and length of rig tube onto the reel line. (3) Now add the supplied lead clip in the same manner. (4) Next, tie on the appropriate boom section for the lead used. (5) Make sure you use the right lead for the system, and add it to the lead clip. (6) Push the tail rubber in place and then push the half swivel into the rubber grommet on the lead. (7) Add the hooklength of your choice, and cover the clip with a sleeve. (8) The COG system is now ready to go, and as you can see, the taking carp will feel the full weight of the lead.

CHOD/HELICOPTER RIGS

Rotary rigs, as they were once called, were one of the very first presentations designed solely with anti-tangle properties in mind, and then other benefits were discovered. Put simply, the hooklink swivel rotates on your reel line or leader, the lead is on the end, and on the cast the hooklink spins due to air pressure, stopping it tangling. These rigs have become very popular with anglers and were predominantly used on leadcore and ultimately led to the birth of the Chod Rig. Thanks to forward-thinking tackle manufacturers, there are various ways of setting up a safe and effective Helicopter arrangement due to the availability of some clever moulded beads that hold the

hooklink in place, but will easily slide off the leadcore in case of a breakage. This presentation is well suited to lakes that are silty, or have some form of bottom weed or debris, in that the top stop on the leadcore can be adjusted to suit

the depth of the lakebed covering.

This presentation is now also the basis for the Chod Rig, which many of you will have seen in this form but might not be as familiar with the now commonly used on-the-line version revealed next.

NAKED CHOD/HELICOPTER RIGS

We aren't really sure how this presentation came about but suspect that it was because so many people wanted to use the Chod Rig but their venues banned the use of leadcore. It is exactly the same only it

doesn't utilise the use of any sort of leader, and is predominantly used on fluorocarbon or sinking mono. Once again, purpose-designed beads now allow anglers to safely create this rig. In the accompanying step-by-step guide we have used Fox products to tie the rig but should

explain there are other types available. One final point, the Chod Rig is often used in weed and some of the modern versions allow the lead to come off under pressure, a feature that we find invaluable.

↙ Naked Chod and Helicopter presentations, where the hooklink is fished directly on the main line rather than a leader, have become very popular.

↓ Some companies have manufactured systems specifically designed for fishing hooklinks directly on the main line.

TEN WORLD RECORDS

ENOUGH SAID!

KRYSTON

Inventors of the High Strength Braid and World Leaders of Hooklength Technology.

WWW.KRYSTON.COM

33

CHAPTER 5

KNOTS
THE WEAKEST LINK

Here is a quick guide to tying just about every knot you'll ever need, whether it's for adding a leader to the reel line, attaching a hook, or even securing a bait, we have something for every eventuality.

Knots aren't witchcraft; with a little patience they are easily mastered, and by following the advice in this chapter you'll be able to identify the correct one to use for the job in hand. Read through each section carefully, and practise tying the knots at home. Really test their strength to the limit to make sure they are suitable for the rig material you have chosen. Before you start here are five tips that will result in a better and stronger knot.

1 Always moisten every knot before bedding it down. Simply use saliva, which will lubricate the material and prevent it 'burning' and weakening as you tighten the knots down.

2 Draw the knots together slowly, rather than yanking them into place, as most knots require being gently teased into position.

3 Always test the knots. Give them a decent pull to ensure they are correct and up to the task ahead. After all, you don't want to lose the carp of a lifetime because of a poor knot.

4 Always check the materials being used are strong, and haven't been weakened in any way. This is especially vital when it comes to the reel line, which should be examined frequently.

5 Keep practising until you get your knots right; it is worth it in the long run. If you have any problems just ask a mate to point you in the right direction, it really is that simple.

KNOTLESS KNOT

This extremely simple knot is probably the most popular knot in carp-angling history. It truly revolutionised carp fishing, offering a way of tying a Hair for your baits as a continuation of a knot to attach your chosen hook pattern. It's strong, and the length of the Hair can be adjusted to suit your own preferences or bait size.

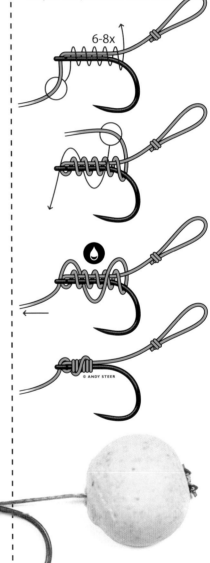

6-8x

© ANDY STEER

OVERHAND LOOP

This knot can be quickly tied, and is perfect when tying stiff mono materials in a hooklink, as it offers the rig more movement. It can also be used to form a loop in coated braid, but check that your chosen material is compatible with this knot as some are severely weakened by it. Another major benefit is that this loop can be used with all materials in conjunction with a quick-change stick clip system.

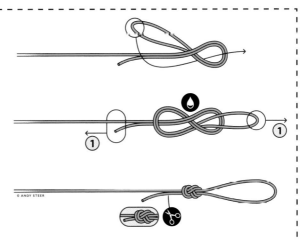

TUCKED BLOOD KNOT

This proven knot has been in use for decades, and according to Ian 'Chilly' Chillcott, is perfect for all applications. It's one of the quickest knots to tie, and is extremely simple. It works especially well with monofilament and is a great way of joining your reel line to your rig. It also works well when tying knots in high-memory mono for Chod Rigs or Hinged Stiff presentations. To get the best results you have to reduce the number of turns, three is normally the best. Be careful when teasing the knot down and make sure that the knot is fully lubricated, which helps to prevent kinking.

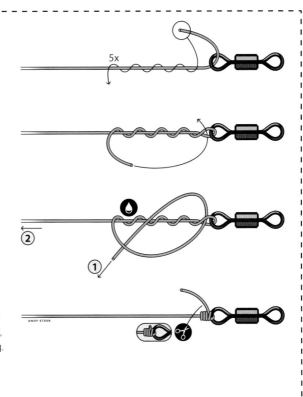

GRINNER KNOT

The Grinner Knot is a firm favourite with many anglers, including me! It can be used for attaching swivels and hooks, as well as being a useful way of attaching a buoyant hookbait to avoid piercing. It gets its name from the fact that it looks like a row of smiling teeth when completed – a happy knot!

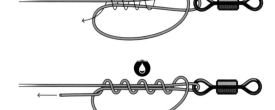

PALOMAR KNOT

This is another knot that is regularly used by some of the top names in carp fishing. Super-strong with virtually every material, the Palomar should never let you down.

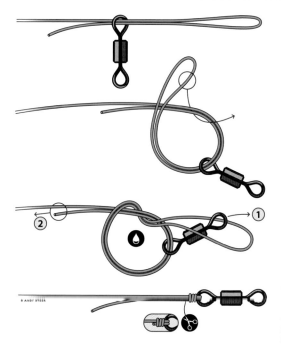

36

CARP RIG: THE MECHANICS

POP-UP ATTACHMENT

You may have seen many anglers tying their pop-up baits onto a running rig ring. This is the knot being used, and it helps prevent the bait being pierced, meaning it will be popped up for longer periods.

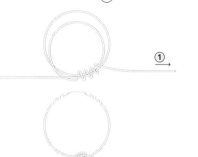

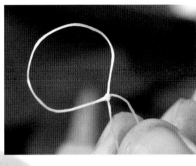

STOP KNOT

This simple knot is one that simply needs to be mastered. It's perfect when marking your lines with pole elastic or marker braid, and literally takes seconds to tie. Ideal on your marker and spod rods, as well as your actual fishing rods.

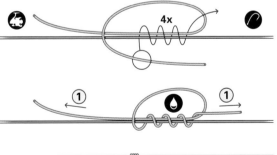

3 cm   3 cm

LEADER KNOT

This knot is, quite simply, fantastic when used in conjunction with thick monofilament shockleader materials. It's painfully simple, and one of the quickest shockleader knots you will ever tie. Get on it.

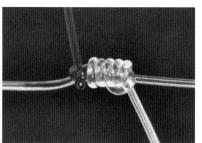

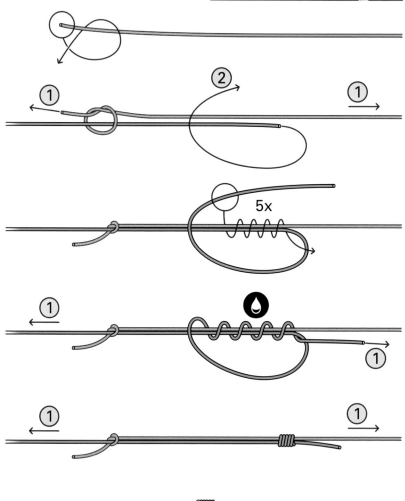

© ANDY STEER

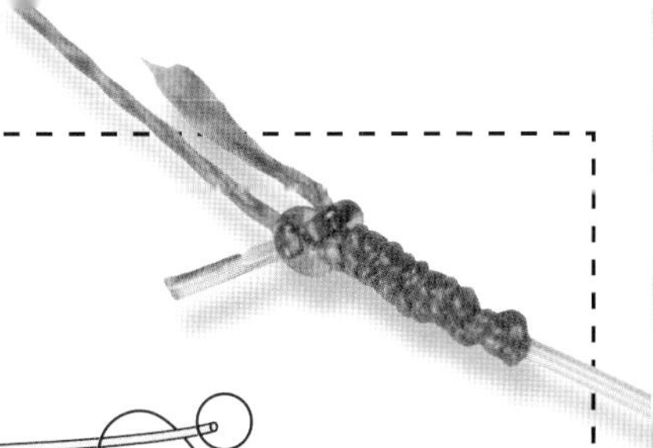

MAHIN KNOT

This particular knot is fast becoming one of the most popular, and there are several different versions of it. Once mastered it is very strong, suits most materials and is even slightly tapered for easy passage through the rod rings.

10x
6x
1
1
2
1
1
© ANDY STEER

Shockleader knots should be placed at the back of the spool, with a minimum of three turns around the spool above the knot. This ensures that the line will leave the spool smoothly on the cast.

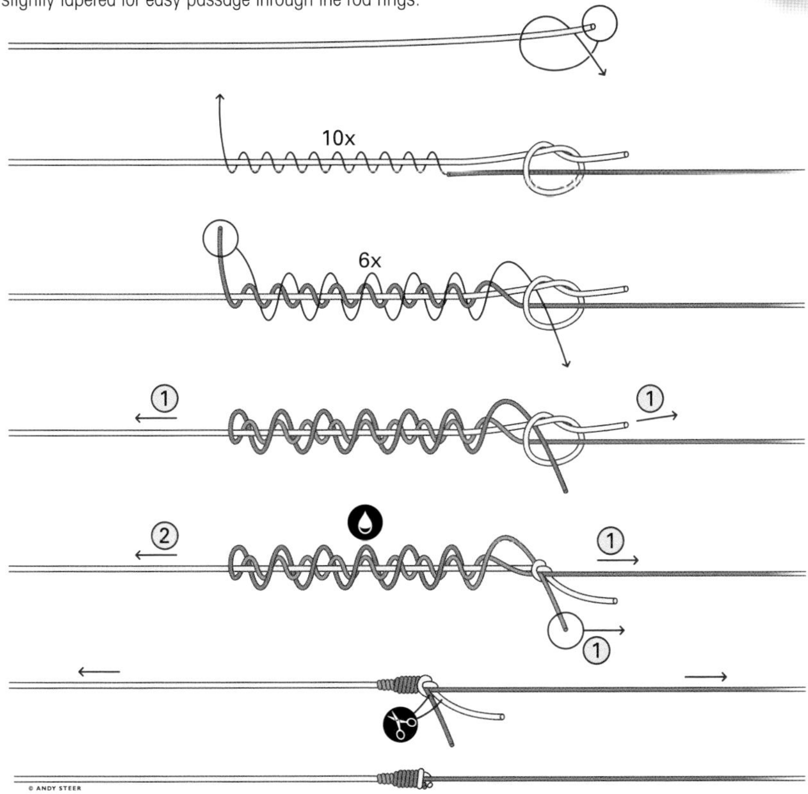

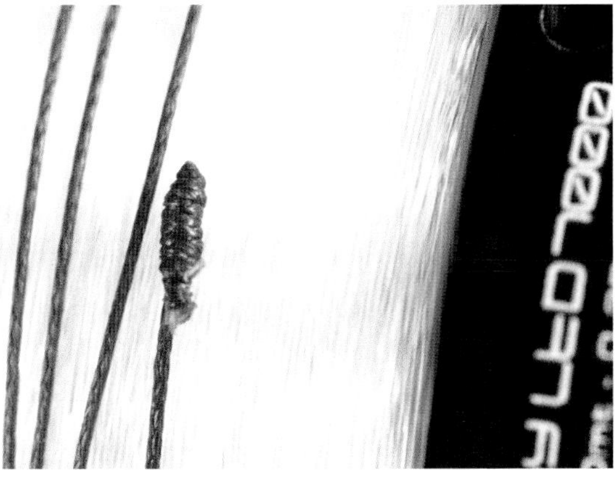

CAN YOU AFFORD NOT TO TRY IT?

ESSENTIAL BOILIES

Weight	15mm	18mm
10kg	£35	£35
20kg	£59	£59
30kg	£69	£69

*All Baitology products are shelf life.

15 FLAVOURS
MATCHING POP-UPS & DIPS FOR BOTH RANGES

PREMIUM BOILIES

Weight	12mm	15mm	18mm
5kg	£30	£27.50	£25
10kg	£59	£54	£49
15kg	£84	£79	£72
20kg	£114	£103	£94
25kg	£140	£126	£115
30kg	£165	£149	£135

High quality, great value boilies from europe's leading bait manufacturer.

ORDER OVER 30KG AND GET FREE MATCHING DIP AND POP-UP

Baitology
Fish with confidence

FRESH PRODUCTS   ATTRACTIVE PRICES   POSTAGE FREE*
*Buy 10kg and more

WWW.BAITOLOGY.COM

CHAPTER 6
HOOKLINKS
MAKING THE RIGHT CHOICE

When it comes to choosing the right hooklink material you would be forgiven for getting confused, simply because the range of different products available is just mind-blowing. Many companies will have a number of different hooklink materials designed to perform very specific tasks and ultimately the final choice is down to you. But which one should you choose?

"It is fair to say that Dave Chilton, of Kryston, is the father of the hooklink revolution"

Thirty years ago, carp rigs were very much a dark art and every successful angler guarded their presentation with a zeal that the modern generation of carpers would shake their head at in disbelief. It is fair to say that Dave Chilton, of Kryston, is the father of the hooklink revolution when he started to market a range of different materials suitable for anglers to use. In those early years, from the late-1980s, it is doubtful whether you would have opened a single tackle box anywhere in the country and not found a spool or two of Kryston's products.

Jump to the modern day and you are now faced with a bewildering array of materials, but don't panic! In reality, the choice of hooklink is fairly basic and you are only faced with a few alternatives to get you on your way. These decisions revolve mainly around how you want your bait and hook to behave once attached to your rig, or, put very simply, this is the choice between stiff, supple, or thin.

To help you understand how each material works, and in what situations you may wish to use them, we have included a brief general description of several different types of hooklink. Be assured that virtually every rig that has ever been cast out will be attached to one or other of these materials in one form or another. Fashion dictates that some will be currently in vogue because certain presentations become popular, but when you look at the guest chapters included in this book, you'll discover that many anglers rely on the same basic presentations that have worked for them for several years.

SOFT UNCOATED BRAIDS

Fly line backing, or more precisely, Dacron, was probably the first supple braid to be used, but it evolved into the range of materials commonly based on Dyneema fibres, as anglers began to search for stronger and more reliable products. These soft and supple materials are an ideal way of creating rigs which act very naturally underwater and allow lots of hookbait movement. Sinking braids are also less conspicuous because their very nature allows them to follow the contours of the lakebed and blend in with their surroundings. On the downside, the very same properties that make them good to use create their own problems, the most obvious being that braid can tangle very easily. This is easily rectified by the use of PVA which not only limits tangles to virtually nil, but actually also makes the rigs land and sit better on the bottom. The popular use of solid PVA bags where your entire rig is enclosed in the confines of the bag lends itself to the use of these supple braids.

COATED BRAIDS

Kryston was definitely the first manufacturer to market a coated braid, and its versatility soon made it immensely popular. Now there are a whole host of different products available. Coated braids are, as their name suggests, a supple braid encapsulated in a tough removable coating. This creates a very user-friendly, adaptable material that is easy to use, virtually tangle-free, very durable, and allows the angler to create a variety of different presentations. Originally, one of the downsides of this type of material was how it would sit and how it appeared on the lakebed. The stiff and thick nature made it very visible and in certain circumstances it can sit up off the lakebed. Manufacturers soon addressed this by producing a range of different coated braids to suit certain circumstances; this includes super-stiff varieties that are ideal for distance casting right through to exceptionally supple materials that sink and lie perfectly on the bottom. The visual nature of coated braids has also been addressed and many now come in very drab camouflage finishes that make them hard to detect. Coated braids are exceptionally versatile and should not be ignored; they form the basis of many easy-to-create and successful rigs.

"A supple braid encapsulated in a tough removable coating"

Stripping coated hooklinks can be a fiddly task, with many people struggling to use their fingernails or even teeth to remove the tough outer coating. Save yourself the drama and use one of the purpose-designed stripping tools produced by many of the top tackle companies.

← Here, you can clearly see two very distinct ways of taking advantage of the properties of coated hooklinks.

STIFF LINKS, NYLON, AND FLUOROCARBONS

Back in the mists of time, stiff rigs were very popular for presenting bottom baits over areas of flat lakebed where the line could lie flush to the bottom. Although not very subtle, these presentations were very difficult for the carp to deal with. From this point, people started to experiment with different materials and the use of stiff fluorocarbon gathered momentum. As discussed in the reel line section, this product has a number of properties which make it the ideal hooklink material; it is stiff, sinks like a brick, and is almost invisible underwater. Fluorocarbons also moved on a step with the introduction of softer versions which help to create more supple and subtle presentations which are favoured by many anglers. The stiff rig then spawned a couple of noted variants that started to use what is termed 'high-memory mono' to create very specialised presentations, the Hinged Stiff Rig and Chod Rig. Both of these rely on the fact that high-memory mono, once heat is added, either via steam

or friction from your fingers, can be manipulated into any shape, from being dead straight to having a distinct curve, and once left to cool retains this shape. This allows anglers to create not only arrow-straight rigid boom sections for their Hinged Stiff Rigs but also aggressively curved hooklinks for the Chod Rig. Finally, there are a number of nylon lines that have become popular for several different presentations. These are classed as pre-stretched lines that are very thin for their stated breaking strain and are ideal for Zig and floater fishing. These products have to be treated with respect because they are hard to knot correctly, and because of their lack of stretch, playing fish on them needs to be a careful process.

↑ Many monofilament hooklinks, especially the high-memory ones, benefit from being steamed over a hot kettle. You can do this to either straighten them, or to set a curve in them.

SPECIALISED HOOKLINKS

That is a brief rundown of the most popular types of hooklink materials that are available, but you will also come across some unique products. There are hooklinks that have a stiff inner section, with a soft braided outer where you can remove the inner core to create your rig. You may even come across materials that have elastic properties once immersed in water and which create a very different type of rig, whereby pressure is applied to the hook. Finally, the more anglers seek out their quarry in a wider range of habitats, the more they come across extreme fishing situations where ultra-strong tackle is required, whether it is needed to defeat the environment or nuisance species such as crabs or crayfish. In these situations ultra-tough hooklink materials are needed, such as Solar Unleaded, Kryston Quicksilver or Fox Armadillo.

→ Multi-Strand is an old-school material which can be fiddly for the novice rig-tier, but offers very subtle presentation options to those who master it.

↓ Martin Locke uses Solar's Unleaded to create what he calls his Kebab Rig.

Multi-Strand was one of the original very supple specialist hooklinks. It provides an almost infinite amount of possiblities when it comes to creating your own unique presentations.

OFFERING VALUE FOR MONEY WITHOUT COMPROMISING ON QUALITY

END TACKLE AND HAND-SHARPENED HOOK SPECIALISTS

"Rig It Tackle worked their magic on my SSC's, the end result absolutely blew me away."
Bill Cottam

Rig Tube | Green | 2m x 0.75mm

RIG-IT TACKLE
SKIN-TECH
Sinking Coated Braid
15lb
20 metres
BROWN
www.rigittackle.com

RIG-IT TACKLE
Tail Rubbers | Brown | Qty 10

RIG-IT TACKLE
Anti-Tangle Sleeve | Brown | Qty 20

RIG-IT TACKLE
Tail Rubbers | Green | Qty 10

RIG-IT TACKLE
CLEAR-TECH
Fluoro Carbon
15lb 35mm
30 metres
CLEAR

RIG-IT TACKLE
Tungsten Putty
BROWN
20g

RIG-IT TACKLE
R1 | Hand Sharpened | Wide Gape Hooks

RIG-IT TACKLE
R2 | Hand Sharpened | Wide Gape Hooks

RIG-IT TACKLE
R3 | Hard | Curved Shank | Hooks

Visit our website to find your local stockist or order direct at www.rigittackle.com

T 07722 881 823
E rigittackle@gmail.com

RIG-IT TACKLE

CHAPTER 7

A BARBED ISSUE
CHOOSING THE RIGHT HOOK FOR YOUR RIG

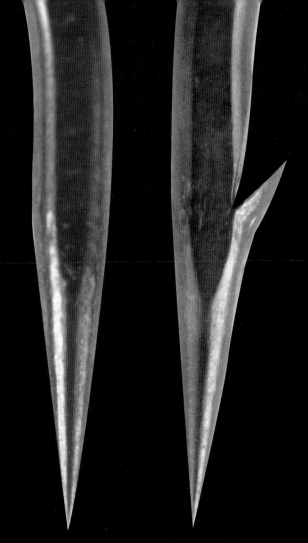

Fishing hooks have a long history dating back to 3,000 BC, when they bore very little resemblance to their modern-day counterparts. It was only in relatively recent times that they became mass-produced and look like the products we use today. For the carp angler the hook is vitally important because not only is it the direct point of contact with his quarry, it has also become a vital rig component thanks to the self-hooking arrangements many use. The choice of hook is virtually limitless, although now there are many specific designs that have been adapted to – or, in some cases, invented specifically for – carp fishing. Anglers will always have their preferred patterns even though there are basic styles that should be used with certain types of presentation.

First, we'll look at what we actually need from a hook and explain some of the major characteristics.

Your hook will always need to be as sharp as possible so that it can penetrate the flesh of the carp's mouth with maximum effect, to attain a good hold. This point is vital and you should always check your hookpoint for sharpness, even with hooks new out of the packet, as transport and mass production can lead to the occasional flaw. The hook also needs to be strong so that it retains its shape during the fight, and ultimately stays in place. There are certain characteristics that should be noted. Straight-pointed hooks prick the carp quickly, whereas a beaked point isn't as efficient but does tend to keep a firmer hold, and it is less likely to blunt. Hooks with an in-turned eye or curved shank also tend to turn quickly, providing good positive holds.

But before we go on to discussing hook patterns, we need to address the barbed versus barbless debate. For many this will be a decision made simply to abide by fishery rules, on other venues anglers will have the freedom of choice. Some believe that barbed hooks hold their position and so do less damage, while others debate that because they are harder to remove; this is the moment when unfortunate mistakes can be made. All we can suggest is that you always carry a set of pliers that are capable of cutting the shank of a hook if necessary, forceps to aid your grip and control during the unhooking process, and some form of antiseptic to treat any minor injuries.

LONGSHANK

This style of hook is very distinctive and crosses several different styles of fishing, including sea and game, although some branded versions are specific to carp. There are several slight variations but predominantly they have a slightly in-turned eye and a straight point. These hooks are known for their ability to turn and prick very quickly, making them useful for a variety of presentations. In order to get the best from this pattern, it is often best to use some form of kicker which helps it turn even more and increases the gape of the hook. As its name suggests, this pattern has a long shank which also benefits from either a small ring added to the Hair or a piece of silicone to hold everything in place. This pattern is very versatile and is at home with either pop-ups or bottom baits.

WIDE GAPE

Again, another truly classic pattern that really has stood the test of time, and which comes in a variety of slightly different guises. This style of hook is probably the most popular and commonly used today due to the fact that it can be used in a number of presentations. You will find it with both an in-turned eye and point, or a straight point and eye, or a mixture of the two. Smaller sizes of patterns with a straight point and eye have proved to be very popular for Zig and floater fishing. The main features of a wide gape pattern are that the shank is normally of medium length, with popular styles for bottom bait fishing having a slightly in-turned eye which, once again, is improved by the addition of a kicker to increase turning potential. These hooks are popular with either type of point configuration and will suit bottom bait or pop-up arrangements. Patterns with in-turned points have proved popular with river carpers because they hold their point in spite of moving around on the riverbed. Super-strong patterns in thick wire gauges are also available for more extreme situations.

POP-UP/CHOD HOOKS

This is a difficult pattern to describe because there is a degree of difference from one manufacturer to another, but the one thing that they all have in common is the out-turned eye. These hooks have evolved relatively recently to keep up with rig trends, more specifically Hinged Stiff Rigs and Choddies, although these patterns are now so popular they are being used in a variety of presentations. This type of hook normally has a wide gape, angled shank, out-turned eye, and, in most cases, a straight point. When tied as part of a pop-up presentation they create an aggressive angle designed to prick the fish very quickly as it sucks in your buoyant hookbait. This pattern of hook is now often used with Multi-Rigs, stiff presentations, and even coated hooklinks where the coating has been left intact. This is a must-have pattern in any angler's box and there are excellent versions by a number of manufacturers.

CURVED SHANK

This group of hooks can be split into two very distinct categories, simply short- or long-shanked. The longshank version has probably created more controversy than anything else in carp fishing, and is said to cause double hooking on some occasions. This has led to it becoming less and less popular in the UK, but it remains a firm favourite abroad. The more popular shorter version can be used in a whole range of popular rigs including the Blowback, KD, 360, plus numerous variations. Its main attribute is that it is very hard to eject due to the very aggressive curve in the shank. There is very little need to use shrink tube with this pattern because its natural shape means that it turns quick and easily does its job of grabbing a hookhold.

As you can see there is a huge overlap between different styles of hook, so we've tried to keep the descriptions simple. We will be more specific when discussing rigs in depth in future chapters.

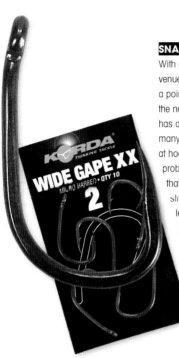

SNAG HOOKS

With anglers facing more extreme venues and conditions and, up to a point, bigger and bigger carp, the need for heavy-duty hooks has arisen. With this in mind, many companies started to look at hook design to combat this problem. They created patterns that have thick, forged wire for strength, short-to-medium-length shanks, ultra-sharp points and large eyes. Once the shank gets over a certain length it can have a tendency to bend, so these are kept fairly short. The thicker the wire, the worse the penetration, so the point needs to be as sharp as possible to get the best results, which is where chemical sharpening makes a huge difference. The large eye is also very important because when this type of hook is needed the strength of hooklink normally goes up as well, so you need the bigger eye to pass the hooklink material through. Although many of these hooks were designed with the Continental angler in mind, they do have uses in the UK too. They are suitable for snag fishing or when heavy weed is present, and many people who fish running water for carp put their faith in this type of hook.

HAND SHARPENED HOOKS

There are many big-name anglers out there who swear by hand-sharpening their hooks but it does take time and practice to get it right and this is where buying your hooks already 'fettled' can make sense. Rig-It Tackle sell their own brand of hooks (sharpened or un-sharpened), which are great value, but you can also order virtually any brand, size and style of hooks from them and they'll arrive on your doormat hand sharpened and ready to use straight from the pack. Some styles and shapes of hook are easier to work on than others, and this is where a professional service can make all the difference but you can rest assured that every hook in every pack will be as sharp as possible and, if you take the trouble to check your current hooks we bet you'll find one or two in most packs that are not quite as sharp as others. This won't happen if you use a professional sharpening service. Remember that the sharpness of your hook is, quite possibly, the most important aspect of your rig, so you need to know this is one aspect you don't need to worry about!

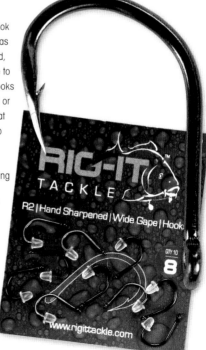

HOOK-SHARPENING

When I get a packet of hooks, I have a look at them straight from the pack and think there may be two or three that are a little less sharp than the others. Due to the fact that hooks are mass produced in their tens of thousands and are handled many times along the way in the process, the points are going to blunt a little. They may feel sharp, but there's sharp and there's sticky-sharp. The final handling process is when 10 or so hooks go into the packet; they sit on the shelves and when in transport rub alongside each other, so it's inevitable that some points are going to be lost a little. This is the reason why some companies are now packaging their hooks in boxes, which separates them and protects the points. Although our fingertips become hardened over time, and have less feeling than a young child's fingertips, we can still tell the difference

between a sharp hook and a hook that has been blunted slightly when it's pressed into a fingertip. Throw into the equation a hookpoint which has been sharpened like the one pictured on this page, and there's an even bigger difference. Just be careful and have the plasters ready!

Actually sharpening hooks from the packet is an acquired skill, and one which takes plenty of practice to refine. Some of the best anglers who sharpen every hook have got this down to a fine art, which it is. I'll be honest here, when I first had a go I didn't do a particularly good job on my first attempt, but three or four hooks later I was well into the groove. I got some pleasing results, with hooks sharper than I'd seen or used before. Now I've got it sussed, there are even some hooks that I would usually discard from the packet that I can actually resurrect.

With hook-sharpening being in

vogue, and something which, in my eyes, results in less missed opportunities, the guys at Taska, Fox, and Gardner have all brought out hook-sharpening tools.

➜ A number of companies market hook-sharpening tools, such as this one from Taska, which comes with a coarse sharpening stone.

↓ Some sharpening stones, such as the Point Doctor from Gardner, are designed for fine-tuning hookpoints, rather than greatly altering them.

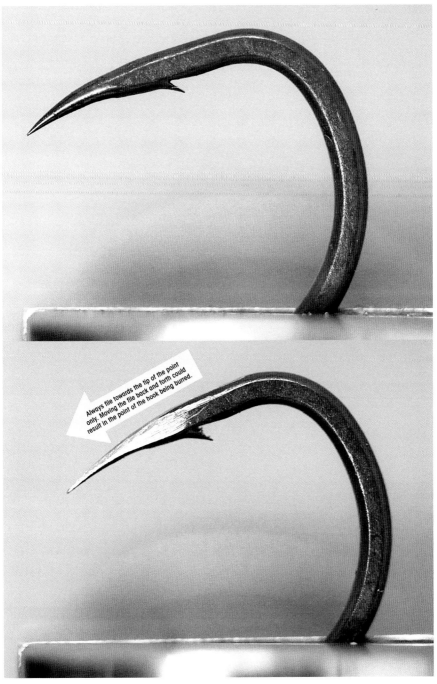

Always file towards the tip of the point only. Moving the file back and forth could result in the point of the hook being burred.

↑ This hookpoint has been transformed from sharp to razor-sharp quickly and easily using a combination of a file and finishing stones. The longer, finer point should prick and penetrate the flesh of a carp's mouth quicker than a standard out-of-the packet hook, which should lead to a better hookhold.

57

CHAPTER 8

ON THE DECK
BOTTOM BAIT RIGS

58

Going back through the mists of time and you'll only really find one type of presentation in carp fishing and that was free-lining; where the weight of the bait was not only used to cast but also to hold itself in position. The belief was that if carp felt any resistance they'd drop the bait. Fishing in this way was very poor and anglers soon started to add weight to hold their rig in place on the lakebed and cast longer distances. This was the birth of what we now call bottom bait rigs. This type of arrangement has accounted for a huge number of carp over the last four decades and is just as relevant today as it was all that time ago. The reality is that carp spend a big part of their time feeding right on, or even in the debris of, the lakebed, so it makes sense to present a bait exactly where they are feeding. With that in mind, let's consider the best rigs for presenting a bait hard on the deck to use this to our full advantage. This type of setup can be fairly basic as you'll see, or more advanced, but they all follow the same basic principles and need to be in your armoury for you to achieve consistent success.

The palm test is when you lay a hooklink across the palm of your hand with the hookbait over one side. You then gently pull the hooklink to see if the hook turns and grabs the flesh on the edge of your hand. This test isn't exact but is a rough guide to how your rig works. It doesn't work with buoyant bait presentations like the KD rig because it isn't supported in water.

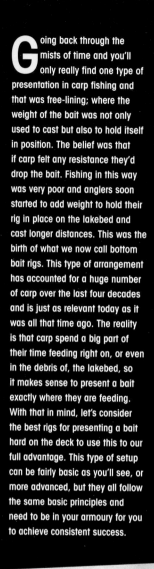

← A proper old-school rig, but if you look closely, you will actually notice not a great deal has changed in over 30 years.

LIGHT MONO RIG

This is probably the oldest of what we would describe as a modern setup, and is basically a hook tied straight onto the end of a normal piece of nylon line. It is often fished fairly long, with 45cm being about right for most situations, but fine-tuning can be undertaken and it can be used drastically shorter or longer if required. The use of normal line means that it has semi-stiff properties, which results in it being tangle-free over most distances, apart from extreme range. It is very easy to tie and works in a large range of different circumstances. Anglers have changed the rig slightly in recent years by using light fluorocarbon in the 10-12lb bracket, which makes the rig virtually invisible underwater. In this instance we have used 12lb nylon, tied a small loop in one end and mounted a 15mm boilie on it. We then go through the eye of a wide gape pattern hook, towards the bend, and position the bait so there is a separation of about 10mm. Then whip up the shank of the hook until level with the hookpoint, before going back through the eye. With the mono being fairly flexible the hook sits correctly but has just enough of a curve, which is enhanced by the in-turned eye of the hook to help the rig to turn. That's it really, a simple rig that can be used on anything from a running lead to a Helicopter Rig.

↓ A new take on an old classic.
A straight fluorocarbon hooklink.

59

STIFF RIGS

If this book had been written 10 years ago, there would have been an entire chapter on Stiff Rigs, but fashion changes and this very effective rig has somewhat fallen out of favour. This is a real pity because it was devastatingly effective then, just as it still is today. The original presentation was fished very short, between 7.5 and 15cm, and was used over areas of the lakebed that were firm/ hard and clean, such as gravel, sand, or clay. Obviously, if the lakebed was soft or had any form of debris on it, the rig could come to rest awkwardly on the bottom, stick up at a funny angle, and ruin the presentation. It can be tied in a variety of ways, all of which stick to the same basic principle, and all of which use stiff materials for the main hooklink, anything from heavy fluorocarbon through to high-memory monofilament. Here are the two versions we like.

The first version is easy; tie a small loop on the end of a piece of your chosen stiff rig material, then mount a bait on the end before adding a longshank hook. You want a gap of at least 5 to10mm between

the bend of the hook and the bottom of the bait, then tie a standard five-turn Knotless Knot. Decide how long you want the rig, again remembering it is more effective short, before tying it to a ring swivel or joined to a normal swivel with a large loop knot, and you are ready to go. A similar presentation is also used but the stiff Hair is cut off and replaced by a flexible Hair, utilising braid to give the bait a bit more movement. The hook pattern can also be varied, with many experienced anglers preferring to use a hook style with an out-turned eye. Many people also use the very new super-stiff coated braids with only the inner core exposed above the hook knot – the choice is yours. This rig is virtually tangle-free so is great for long-range fishing, can be used Helicopter-style or with a lead clip, and it is fairly guaranteed that the fish in your lake won't have seen it for ages.

> **This rig is virtually tangle-free so is great for long-range fishing**

Two rigs, same principle, different construction. The top rig features a pre-formed kicker, a small piece of silicone to trap the Hair against the shank of the hook, and a purpose-designed sinker, whereas the bottom rig features a shrink tube kicker, a rig ring keeping the Hair tight to the shank, and a blob of tungsten putty to keep it pinned to the deck.

BRAID OR SOFT-COATED BRAID RIG

The actual style of these rigs is identical, it is only the material from which it is tied that varies and that is down to personal choice. Lots of anglers are afraid to use soft braids because if used incorrectly they can tangle easily. Braid is good to use because it is so limp; it can follow the contours of the lakebed, sit over low-level bottom debris, and can lie correctly even if the lead has dug in soft silt. Adding sinkers or blobs of putty enhances this. Tangles can be virtually 100% eradicated by using some form of PVA, either a stringer or small mesh bag. Soft-coated braids are a little less prone to tangling and are preferred by many anglers; adding sinkers or putty also helps the lie of the hooklink.

If using coated braid, strip several centimetres of

the coating, apart from this the technique is the same, regardless of material. Tie a small loop in the end of the braid before threading on a small rig ring, which is tied in place roughly 15-20mm from the loop, depending on the size of bait. Or add a small piece of thin silicone tubing that is then pushed over the hookpoint to sit in a similar position to the rig ring (see picture). Then tie a simple Knotless Knot, leaving a 1-1.5cm gap to where the coating starts if using coated braid. Next you can either add a short length of shrink tube or one of the purpose-made kickers/line-aligners produced by many companies. If you use shrink tube you'll have to steam it to shape, if not you are ready to go. Again, this presentation can be used in conjunction with a wide variety of lead arrangements, although our favourite is the lead clip.

62

CHAPTER 9

FEATHER-LIGHT
CRITICALLY-BALANCED PRESENTATIONS

Slow-sinking, or balanced baits are the same presentation, and that's a bait and rig that has been fine-tuned to sink slowly under just the weight of the hook, or with the aid of a tiny bit of added ballast via a split shot or putty. The aim is to get a presentation that sits on or very near to the lakebed. This serves a variety of functions, the first being that the bait and rig behaves more like a free offering, making it harder for the carp to

distinguish what is safe to eat and what is attached to a rig. The second property is the fact that this inherent buoyancy means that the bait and rig enters the fish's mouth easily and quickly when sucked in, making it even harder for the carp to deal with the rig, and resulting in better hookholds. This is a very subtle type of rig that is far less blatant than a pop-up, and which has accounted for the capture of countless numbers of carp.

HOOKBAIT CHOICE

The first thing you need is a bait with some buoyancy and this is available in a variety of forms: a wafter which is a purpose-designed slow-sinking bait, a Snowman arrangement that utilises a pop-up to negate the weight of a bottom bait, fake corn which is available in a range of densities, or by adding a cork insert into a standard boilie. All have exactly the same effect – a hookbait which, once the rig is attached, sinks very slowly to the bottom and sits gently over any type of bottom, even a covering of light weed. There are several rigs that suit this presentation and here are three of the most commonly used, but there are lots of different variations.

THE KD RIG

This rig is suitable for a wide range of different angling situations and has been very popular over the last few years. It is equally at home presenting a bait over a scattering of boilies as it is over a spodded area, or even with a PVA bag. There are two styles of hooks that lend themselves to this presentation:

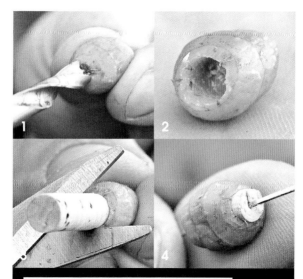

HOW TO CRITICALLY-BALANCE A TIGER NUT

Start by taking a nut drill and carefully bore in to the centre of a tiger nut (1) until you have created a neat hole that goes about three-quarters of the way into the nut (2). Now insert a cork stick and trim with scissors (3) so that the cork is flush with the edge of the nut. Finally, mount on the Hair by pushing a baiting needle through the centre of the cork, exiting out of the other side of the nut (4).

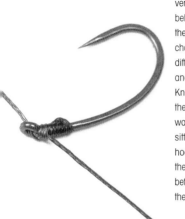

curve shanked models or wide gapes, the choice is yours. The rig is simplicity itself to tie and can also be used with either braid or a coated hooklink depending on your own preference, although we prefer soft-coated braid with a very small section stripped back behind the hook. Add the bait to the hooklink before tying it to your chosen hook; this knot is slightly different to what you are used to and is a derivative of the Knotless Knot. Thread the hooklink through the eye of the hook in the normal way, making sure that the bait is sitting just past the bend of the hook. Then make two turns of the hooklink around the shank before moving the bait to below the eye of the hook. Start to whip

up the shank in the normal way, trapping the Hair between the second and third turns, stopping after seven turns and passing the hooklink back through the eye to complete the knot. If the weight of the hook won't sink the bait on its own, add a shot to the Hair just under the hookbait; this needs to be big enough to sink the bait slowly so that the hook lies flat on the bottom. It works equally as well with boilies, particles or fake corn. This rig is very aggressive, and when the carp sucks it in, the mechanics mean that the eye of the hook becomes light, which means that the hookpoint is heavy and so drops to catch the bottom lip perfectly. A great rig that is very versatile.

Snowman presentations can be created in a wide variety of ways, including putting two half-baits together like this.

A SNOWMAN RIG

You may think that this type of bait presentation is very old hat, but it still catches more than its fair share, and is thought by many to be a big-fish rig, thanks to its track record of catching outsize specimens. This bait arrangement can be used on a variety of different rigs, but once again we will show you how to reproduce our favoured setup. Again, ease is one of the key factors about this rig, yet it still remains a good fish-catcher. We like to use a curved shank hook pattern with a semi-stiff coated hooklink. Strip several centimetres of the hooklink and tie a loop in the end before adding the pop-up and bottom bait; make sure they are the right way round, with the pop-up on top. Tie the hook in place using the Knotless Knot, so that the bait sits just past the hook. Then slide one of the purpose-designed line-aligners or a 2cm piece of shrink tube up the hooklink, before teasing it over the eye, covering the knot and stopping just level with the hookpoint, and then steam if needed. We fish this rig using a Helicopter presentation and find it perfect for fishing over a large spread of boilies. The bait sinks slowly, so is ideal for a variety of different lakebeds, and the Helicopter Rig complements this. Once the bait has come to rest it sits over the hook, making it harder to spot. An awesome presentation that is so simple.

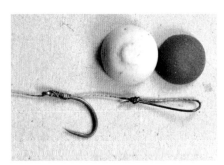

↑ To prevent the bottom bait boilie sliding down the Hair, creating a gap between the bottom bait and the pop-up, a larger loop is required, ensuring that the knot is placed inside the bottom bait.

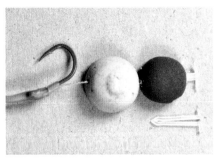

↑ Short Hairs on pre-tied rigs can be elongated using dedicated Hair stops to accommodate a double bait. Ensure that the stop goes right the way through the pop-up and into the bottom bait.

"Artificial baits have proved time and again how effective they are"

FAKE CORN RIG

It is still hard to believe that there are loads of anglers out there who have no faith in plastic corn, or should I say fake hookbaits, because the range of artificials is growing all the time, and have proved time and again how effective they are. Here is a great little setup that works especially well over a spodded area, although lots of carpers use it in conjunction with PVA sticks or small mesh bags. Rest assured that it is devastating. Hooklink-wise, you can use coated or uncoated braid; in this instance we have used braid. Tie a loop in the end of the piece of braid then thread on a grain of

floating corn lengthways, so that the fat end is at the Hair stop. This is because it is the most buoyant end and helps the rig sit correctly. Next, tie a small rig ring in place about 1cm below the base of the corn. Pass the rig ring over the point of a longshank hook so that it's adjacent to the barb, before tying the hook in place using a Knotless Knot. Then add a kicker or short length of shrink tube and steam to shape, and that's it. If you are using it with PVA sticks you will have to incorporate some form of quick-change clip so that it can be threaded in place; lead arrangements can vary.

There are loads of different types of plastic hookbaits to choose from, including boilies, pellets and maggots, and most have a degree of buoyancy, making them ideal for critically-balanced presentations.

FEATHER-LIGHT

CHAPTER 10

OFF THE DECK
POP-UP PRESENTATIONS

Pop-up rigs are great at hooking carp and often achieve perfect hookholds smack bang in the middle of the bottom lip, exactly where you want them. But like all rigs you have to understand precisely when and where to use these devilishly effective rigs. A pop-up stands up off the lakebed, so is ideal for combating weed, silt, and even leaf litter in the autumn. It is a highly visible form of presenting a bait, and as much as it can be a very good way of fishing, it can also sometimes be the kiss of death to sport, so understanding the moods of your water is key to success. When most people think of pop-ups they automatically have single hookbait fishing in mind, but this isn't the be-all and end-all of buoyant baits, and they equally have a place when fishing over beds of baits. All the rigs included in this chapter work in a wide variety of different situations.

67

Pop-up rigs can be the perfect solution to overcome weedy waters. Depending on the depth and thickness of the weed, the correct choice of rig will ensure your hookbait and hook are presented cleanly above the weed.

CHOD AND HINGED STIFF RIGS

You must have spent your time on Mars if you haven't heard of the Chod, but we'll go over it just in case. We've coupled it with the Hinged Stiff Rig because they do go hand in hand. The hooklink section is identical in both setups, and up to a point only the length (the distance the bait is presented off the bottom) is altered. Take a Chod-style hook – there are several on the market – and tie it on using a length of high-memory mono; you can use a Knotless Knot, although some anglers swear by other knots. Take the tag end above the knot and thread on a small ring or a Pop-up Peg before bending it round in a D shape and passing it back through the eye, trim it and blob it with a lighter. Next, tie on a top-quality ring swivel using a two-turn Blood Knot to create a hooklink of roughly between 5-7cms. That is the basic Chod setup, and all you have to do is add a pop-up and either fish it directly on the reel line, a Naked Chod, or mounted on some form of leader. To create a Naked Chod, either slide a special tungsten bead up the line, or a sinker, to which you add a wide bore bead. This should be about 1m from the end, then add the hooklink. The hooklink will need a small piece of tungsten putty moulding round it to help sink the bait; this isn't needed when using a leader because the weight of the leader will sink the presentation. The bottom of the arrangement can be completed

↑ This unique system from Fox enables Chod, Hinged Stiff and Helicopter rigs to be fished at a predetermined distance from the lead, whilst also offering a safety-conscious lead ejection system.

in a range of ways, including specially designed sleeve systems to dump the lead, or buffer beads, all of which work well. Leaders should be set up in the same way, but the bead arrangements need to be of a wider bore to deal with the thickness of the leader material. This rig is best suited to a scattering of boilies over an area of light weed. It is often misused in areas where there is no weed and it isn't necessary.

To turn it into a Hinged Stiff Rig you simply have to add a boom section. This can be tied from the same material as the hooklink for a very stiff boom, or a softer specialised material such as Trick Link, which sits better over lakebed contours, or you can even use unstripped coated braid. The boom should be roughly three to four times longer than the hooklink and can be used in conjunction with a lead clip or Helicopter setup.

> This rig is best suited to a scattering of boilies over an area of light weed. It is often misused in areas where there is no weed and it isn't necessary

↑ A standard Hinged Stiff Rig where the ring swivel sits in the loop.

↑ The short, curved hooklink from the Hinged Stiff Rig is used in the Naked Chod Rig presentation, and slides on the line to be stopped by a bead.

70

MULTI-RIG

This is an arrangement that has seen loads of publicity, thanks to Carpworld's very own Mike Kavanagh, although some people will know it by other names. Again, this is a very versatile setup that really lends itself to fishing pop-ups, although it can be adapted to suit a wide range of situations. It is easy to tie, allows you to change just the hook without retying the rig, and it catches – what more could you want? Form a loop in the end of a piece of coated braid, then slide down a 1cm piece of silicone sleeve, before passing the loop through your preferred hook pattern. Our favourite is a Chod pattern. Then slide a rig ring or swivel onto the loop before passing the end of the loop over the hookpoint, and pull back through the eye to create the perfect D on the back of the hook. To hold this, slide the silicone sleeve up and over the eye, and tie on a pop-up. Break the coating on the hooklink by the knot and reveal 3-4mm of inner core before adding a small split shot. To sink the pop-up perfectly, add putty around the shot until balanced. This can be fished on any lead arrangement, and is a great setup that requires no steaming or messing around. You can even swap the hook, if you need to, by reversing the above process.

→ The Multi-Rig has proved very effective for its inventor Mike Kavanagh over the years. He reckons it's not just great for pop-ups, but for bottom baits and wafters too.

THE WITHY POOL RIG

The brainchild of Steve Renyard, this is a rig that really does outfox those super-wary fish, and has been very prolific for well over 20 years. The presentation, however, has always been a pain to create, a fact that puts many people off using it, which is a real shame considering how good it is. That was until now, when a variety of manufacturers have started to market preformed adaptors that make tying the rig so simple. The rig should always be tied using very supple braid such as Kryston's Silkworm, or a very soft coated braid with a section of coating removed just below the adaptor. Tie on the hook, either a wide gape or curved pattern, then thread on an adaptor and push it over the eye of the hook. Next, thread a small rig swivel or ring down the shank of the hook before pushing a rig stop over the point of the hook. Tie on the pop-up and mould enough putty around the end of the adaptor to sink the bait. This rig turns really well and always grabs the bottom lip for a good hookhold. This really is a great rig made so simple, and you can even get them ready-tied if you are struggling to tie it.

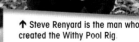

↑ Steve Renyard is the man who created the Withy Pool Rig.

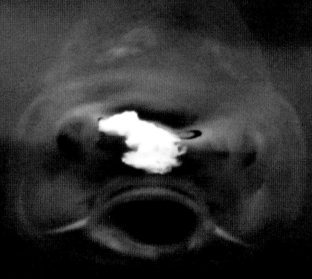

73

CHAPTER 11

ON OR NEAR
THE SURFACE

TARGETING CRUISING CARP

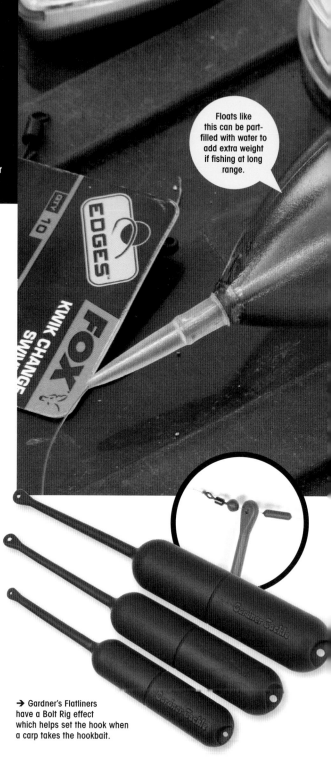

Carp spend a massive amount of their time off the bottom, and many anglers believed that the only way you could catch them was with a floating hookbait. This has all changed in recent years, and the popularity of Zig Rig fishing now means that you can fish effectively for our quarry wherever they are in the water column.

Floats like this can be part-filled with water to add extra weight if fishing at long range.

ON THE TOP

It wasn't so long ago that most people's idea of floater fishing was on a red-hot day when the carp were cruising all over the place. The idea was to break the corner off a stale butty, impale it onto a large hook tied straight to the end of 15lb reel line and chuck it out a rod length, for the bait to immediately fall off. Thank goodness all this has changed.

Floater fishing can be one of the most exciting ways of catching a carp, but the right setup is essential. Basically, you need a reel loaded with a buoyant line; some anglers like normal mono, others prefer braid. We would start with mono of between 8-12lb, depending on the size of fish and nature of the venue, and because it is a bit more user-friendly. Rig-wise, there is very little that is complicated about surface fishing and the presentations are all basically the same. The finesse is derived from the style of float used, hooklink material, and hook size.

Let's start at the float and work our way along the rig. The float serves a variety of functions, it is your casting weight, it can be a visual indicator, not only for when you have a take but also

→ Gardner's Flatliners have a Bolt Rig effect which helps set the hook when a carp takes the hookbait.

for where your bait actually is, and finally, it can also help when it comes to hooking a taking fish. There are a wide variety of styles out there that are the fruition of many hundreds of hours of fishing and design, so you don't really have to worry about choice. The only advice we'd give is to use the smallest controller you need to reach the fish, as subtle can often be the key.

Slide the float onto the line and fix it in place in the appropriate manner, which will be explained in full on the packaging. Next you need to add the hooklink, and this should be made from one of the purpose-designed lines that have been created for Zig and floater fishing. These lines are clear and thin so they are difficult for the carp to see on the surface and distinguish whether the floating bait is attached to anything. Tie a small loop in the end of a 150cm length of line and add the hook using a Knotless Knot. We recommend using a small Size 8 to 12 hook in either a wide gape pattern or a dedicated Zig shape. Then tie the hooklink to the swivel by the float using a Palomar Knot. Mount your chosen bait on the Hair; you can use a range of baits, from a cut-down pop-up to a floating pellet or a drilled dog biscuit, and you are ready. Carp are easy to spook when feeding on the surface, so we recommend that you spend time feeding the swim with floaters to build up confidence before casting out your rig.

← **This useful device from Nash is called a Bread Bomb and is like a bait band combined with a line-aligner; it's great for using bread hookbaits at range.**

ON OR NEAR THE SURFACE

THE ZIG RIG

A Zig is very simple; it is a buoyant hookbait that is presented straight off a lead on a light hooklink, where the bait is fished at a set depth anywhere within the water column. This style of fishing has really come into its own in recent years, with some anglers like Fox's Tom Maker really pioneering the approach and highlighting just how effective it is. In practice the rig is very simple. All you need is a lead clip on the line. It is advisable that the lead comes off, so make sure the tail rubber is only just pushed on; or don't use a rubber, instead tie it in place using PVA tape. We also highly recommend that you use a quick-change-style swivel, which allows you to swap the hooklink quickly. This enables you to have various length pre-tied hooklinks that can be changed easily as you search to find the depth at which the fish are feeding. The hooklinks are identical to those you would use for floater fishing, the only difference being that if you want a bait 30cm off the bottom, you use a hooklink that

Zigs can be a pain to cast, so many experts recommend placing the hookbait on a bucket lid, unhooking mat, or in a cup to cast out. This prevents the hookpoint catching on anything – believe it or not, many top anglers learnt their lesson by accidentally hooking their bivvies, chairs, friends – the list goes on!

↓ Gardner produce a convenient Zig Rig Session Pack which consists of line, foam and hooks.

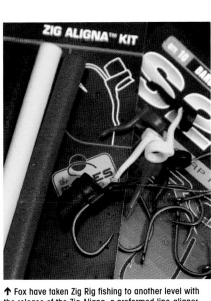

↑ This is how the Zig Aligna sits in the water, mimicking perfectly an emerging caddis fly larva.

↑ Fox have taken Zig Rig fishing to another level with the release of the Zig Aligna, a preformed line-aligner sleeve with a loop on the back to hold foam hookbaits.

↓ Playing fish on long hooklinks with a heavy lead bouncing around can be tricky. Always eject the lead on the take if possible, to avoid potential hookpulls.

long. Bait choice can be a small pop-up or a piece of coloured foam mounted straight on the Hair.

A recent development by Fox is a little gizmo called a Zig Aligna, which really has taken the fishing world by storm, and we really like it. It is a pre-shaped kicker that helps turn the hook, but it also holds a small barrel of foam to create the perfect Zig hookbait. In use, just tie the hook onto the end of the hooklink using a Grinner or Palomar, then slide an Aligna down and over the eye of the hook. Using the special tool, add a piece of foam to the loop on the back of the Aligna and trim to the desired size. These little gadgets come in a variety of colours and are a great way of mounting a foam hookbait; you can even leave the foam soaking in flavour if you want to give it some extra pulling power. Zigs catch loads of fish all year round and 24 hours a day, and although it is a big step to chuck out a piece of foam in midwater and expect it to catch, it really does work and you do need to try it.

THE ADJUSTABLE ZIG

The standard Zig is fine for depths up to about 4m, but anything over that and you start to experience a couple of problems. The first is that casting a 4m or longer hooklink can be a nightmare, just as playing and netting a fish on this length of line can be nerve-racking and difficult, especially when you are on your own. The answer to this is the Adjustable Zig, a technique that allows the angler to fish a bait at any depth thanks to the clever use of a float. The whole setup works in exactly the same way as a marker float, and line is paid out so the float can rise to the chosen depth. There are a few manufacturers that make purpose-designed Zig floats, and here we are using the Fox version.

Thread on the lead link; this helps to combat any bottom debris and allows the float to rise smoothly to the surface. You will need to use a reasonably big lead for the rig to work properly. Next, thread on the float, which is an in-line style, before tying a quick-change-style swivel to the end of the reel line and pulling it in place into the gripped recess in the nose of the float. The hooklink should be around 1m in length.

Then thread on a rig sleeve and tie a small loop in the end to allow you to change rigs quickly.

The technique for using the adjustable Zig is easy. Pinch a piece of dissolving foam around the stem of the float and nick the hookpoint through it – this stops tangles. Next cast out to your desired spot and sink the rig on a tight line, keeping everything taut. Once the rig has settled the hookbait will be roughly 1m off the lakebed, and you can then either pay out line until you position the bait at exactly the depth you want it, or simply let it up 30cm every 30 minutes or so to search the water column. The advantage is that when you get a take you actually end up playing the fish on just a 1m long hooklink, which makes life so much easier, and is a great way of fishing a variety of depths without constant recasting. A setup that is well worth understanding, and you should always have a suitable float in your bag, just in case.

↓ Even though the Adjustable Zig rig uses a float, you still need a super-buoyant hookbait to do the job.

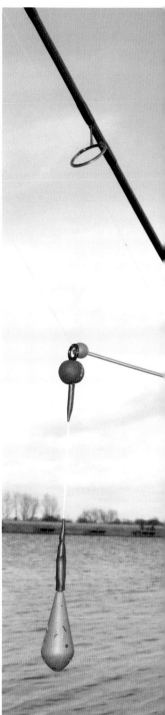

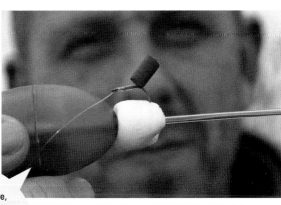

Due to their nature, Adjustable Zigs are prone to tangling on the cast. Nicking your hook into a PVA nugget wrapped around the stem of the float will prevent this.

CHAPTER 12
THE DISSOLVING
MIRACLE
PVA AND ITS MANY USES

Set foot on any lake and take a quick look in virtually any angler's bag and you are bound to find some form of PVA product. But what is it, and where does it come from, and – more importantly –how can we use it to our advantage? Polyvinyl alcohol, or PVA to you and me, is a water-soluble synthetic polymer which has a set of properties that make it ideal for use in fishing. It is resistant to both oil and grease, meaning it can be handled, it dissolves easily, in even relatively cold water, and yet leaves no residue, smell or taste. These traits eventually led to it being used as a bait delivery method for anglers, and the rest, as they say, is history.

PVA is produced in a variety of different forms: string, tape, mesh, and solid PVA bags, and there is even what is described as PVA foam, all of which can be used very effectively when it comes to fishing. There is no doubt that PVA has, in one way or another, changed how many of us fish, and there are anglers out there who rarely, if ever, cast out without having some form of PVA attached.

MESH

PVA mesh is actually knitted yarn, and was made popular by Korda's Danny Fairbrass. It is used in two distinct ways, either to form small round bags that can be nicked on the hook or to form sticks that are threaded down your hooklink to cover your hook. Both tactics are exceedingly effective and result in the capture of thousands of carp on a regular basis. PVA has two main advantages that make it so useful; firstly, you get a nice tight pile of bait right by your hook, and secondly, and just as importantly, your rig rarely tangles.

When using mesh bags there are certain things that need to be considered in order to get the best from them, the main one being the size and resulting impact on the water's surface when you cast your bag out. The larger the bag, the greater the force with which it hits the water, and this can actually dislodge your lead from a lead clip, or move your top bead when using a Helicopter presentation. This can be prevented in two ways;

For ease of use, speed, and efficiency, PVA mesh is hard to beat as a means of presenting a small pile of bait near your rig.

either feather the cast at the point of impact (this should be done automatically, yet many anglers fail to do it), or simply tie the lead in place with PVA tape. When the PVA has dissolved, the lead will be released in the normal fashion. A useful alternative to feathering is to cast clipped up to a predetermined distance, a particularly useful tactic when you are casting to a margin or a hole in the weed.

Sticks have all the plus points of PVA bags, but they really do have a big bonus, in the fact that they mask and protect your hook on the cast. This is especially important when fishing in any form of weed and is a way of ensuring that your presentation is the best it can possibly be. The narrow bore PVA can be used to make very small sticks that are often favoured for distance casting. These prove to be an asset because they keep your hook arrangement in perfect condition during the huge pressures of a big cast, making sure that the Hair can't tangle or twist. All sticks also

One final way of using narrow PVA is with boilies to create an exploding tangle-free stringer

help your hooklink to fall away from the lead as it hits the bottom, which in turn aids presentation.

One final way of using narrow PVA is with boilies to create an exploding tangle-free stringer. Simply tie a small mesh bag with three whole boilies inside, which should be in a triangle shape and as tight as possible. Once knotted, press the middle boilies forward to create three baits all in a line inside the mesh. Then, using a baiting needle, pull the Hair through the boilie in the normal fashion before adding a Hair stop, your hook can then be nicked through the top of the mesh. This creates a

tangle-free presentation where the Hair cannot wrap around the hook. Once in place the PVA contracts as it dissolves and puts pressure on the boilies until they pop out of the PVA, creating a spread of bait.

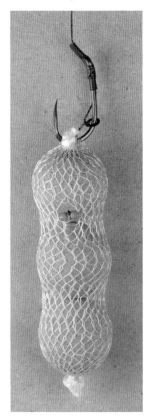

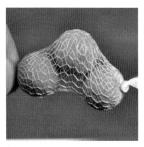

↑ To create an exploding stringer, encapsulate three whole boilies in narrow PVA mesh, tied tightly to create this triangle shape.

↑ Push the middle boilie to get all three baits in a straight line, then push a needle through the end bait at a 45° angle.

↑ Fix the bait in place on the Hair with a boilie stop, and nick the hook through the top of the mesh. The exploding stringer is now ready.

TAPE & STRING

This product is a must have item in your box because it has so many uses, from the simple stringer through to making sure your lead drops off when rig fishing. Thread three boilies onto a 15cm length of tape and position them about an inch apart, then nick your hookpoint through one end of the tape before wrapping it round your hookshank and repeating the process. This traps the Hair in place and eliminates the chance of the Hair tangling, the end result being that you get some free offerings around your hookbait.

If you don't want to use a stringer just tie the Hair in place using a small piece of tape, or you can even use it to mask your hookpoint to minimise the chance of getting a strand of weed impaled. This is the best way of making sure that your rig is sitting perfectly.

There are lots of situations where it isn't necessary to drop the lead or weight, but when Zig fishing it is essential. The problem arises when you are fishing with long hooklinks and a lead clip, in that the take is often not positive enough to cause the lead to fall off. This means that you can end up in the situation where you are playing a fish on a 3m+ hooklink

> **PVA stringers may not be a fashionable tactic to use these days, but no one can deny their effectiveness.**

with a lead swinging on the line, making things very uncomfortable, with the chance that the hookhold will be weakened. So instead, use a lead clip with no tail rubber and secure it in place with PVA tape. This means it is safe to cast, but once the PVA dissolves the

lead will be released every time.

It goes without saying that your hands, tackle, bait and bag contents need to be dry for you to tie and cast PVA setups effectively, but when you are struggling in wet conditions, the addition of salt to your bag contents can make life easier (and enable you to use items like hemp and nuts). Many of the liquid attractors on offer are PVA-friendly. Rest assured that when you use these edges the PVA will dissolve when it is in position in the lake!

PVA can be used for so many different things that we recommend you never leave home without it.

> **Masking the hookpoint and trapping the Hair in place with PVA tape is good practice on every cast.**

Some top carp anglers have taken to using a syringe to inject liquid additives into their solid PVA bags. When the bag melts, the liquids send food signals throughout the water column, grabbing the attention of any nearby carp.

SOLID BAGS

This tactic is absolutely devastating yet still isn't as popular as it should be. The main reason for this is the fact that mastering tying a solid bag is classed as tricky by many, and it can also be difficult if weather conditions are against you. Taking all these things into consideration, it is still a presentation that is definitely worth the effort. Fox produce a very good system called the Rapide Load, which makes tying solid bags very quick and easy. For a better explanation please follow our step-by-step guide, which also reveals how your rig should be added to the bag for the best results.

When you use a solid PVA bag it is essential to get your rig choice absolutely right. We recommend using a short braided hooklink which allows itself to be concertinaed up when at the tying stage. You will also need this to be used with some sort of lead system and, without doubt, an in-line lead is definitely the best. The choice of the venue being fished will dictate whether a drop-off or standard 'on the line lead' should be used. We also suggest the use of short leaders using materials like Unleaded, Submerge, or leadcore with the lead removed. When using bags it is often best to have several tied up in advance so that you can simply add another bag via the loop-to-loop technique rather than waste time tying one.

HOW TO TIE A SOLID PVA BAG

Place your hookbait into the bottom of the bag, cover with 25mm of mix, then lower your lead into the bag **(1)**. Next, add more mix **(2)** until the bag is three-quarters full and nicely compacted **(3)** ensuring there are no trapped air pockets in the bag. Twist the top **(4)** which tightens the entire package, before tying off with PVA tape **(5)**. Press and stick the corners down to create an aerodynamic finished bag **(6)**.

CHAPTER 13
THE MATCH
ANGLER'S FRIEND
MASTERING THE METHOD FEEDER

The Method feeder, as it has booomo known, was once considered to be solely the preserve of the match angler, but specialist carp anglers soon adopted it for their branch of the sport. It was initially designed to be fished on commercial venues with a large head of small carp, and how it was subsequently used changed over the years. To begin with, the feeder was a very similar design to those you see today but the technique was different. A match angler would use two different groundbaits, one hard and one soft. You would create a hard core of groundbait round your feeder and fold your hooklink back into the outer layer of this centre ball. Then you would cover the whole lot again, forming a large, all-encompassing ball surrounding everything. The idea was that on the lakebed the carp would be attracted to the soft groundbait and would start to attack it, creating competition and a feeding frenzy as the ball was whittled away. Eventually the hookbait would be released and grabbed by the unwary carp.

This worked exceptionally well for match anglers but carp anglers needed to approach things a little

↑ Method feeders come in a variety of sizes and different styles.

differently. This was because the time between bites was often a lot longer, so a stiffer mix needed to be used right from the off. The basic technique and setup is still the same but carpers tend to user stiffer mixes. Modern carp feeders are also a lot heavier than their match-fishing counterparts to aid casting and increase the hooking potential. In practice, simply mould an inner core of your groundbait around the frame of your feeder,

then fold your short hooklink and bait back into the feeder, before covering it with more of the mix. The entire ball can then be cast out. If you are using large feeders and casting reasonable distances, to be safe we recommend some form of shockleader. Then, as the mix breaks down, it releases the hookbait and creates a large pile of bait containing your rig. This is very similar to using a large solid PVA bag presentation. This tactic is not only good on venues with a higher stock density, but is also great for dealing with weed; because the feeder is dense and compact and the hooklink is inside, the end tackle will actually punch its way through the underwater foliage.

Although there are lots of variations of feeders they are all basically the same, utilising a frame to hold either your groundbait or dissolving paste,

> **As the mix breaks down, it releases the hookbait and creates a large pile of bait containing your rig**

↑ Here you can clearly see a perfectly-loaded flat feeder, ready to go.

although there are Method leads available too. The one major change that has occurred in recent years is the introduction of giant flat feeders, an idea once again taken from the match-fishing world. These feeders are only weighted on their base and when you add bait, often using a mould, you create a humped ball of bait looking a little like a tortoise's shell (see pic). The advantage of these feeders is that they are very good at holding position on features such as island margins. In addition they are very user-friendly, and the hookbait is always exposed.

Setting up a Method feeder couldn't be easier; although you can use them with some sort of leader there is very little need and we prefer to use them straight on the line, whether this is standard 15lb nylon or a heavy shockleader. (Remember, if you use a braided leader please use

There are various ways of positioning the hookbait when Method fishing. Some prefer it encased within the ball, while others prefer to push it into the outer skin, as shown here.

"This tactic is not only good on venues with a higher stock density, but is also great for dealing with weed"

↑ Critically-balanced corn, or a small 10mm pop-up are the perfect hookbaits to get the best from the Method.

tubing or something similar to protect the fish.) Pass your line through the centre of the feeder before either tying on a swivel or quick-change clip. Then tie on a short braided hooklink, which allows you to easily fold the rig back into the Method ball; we recommend between 75-150mm in length. The hooking arrangement is kept simple, normally a basic Knotless Knot, but we do advise using balanced hookbaits. This is because when the fish drops to feed on the ball of bait, the lighter hookbait should enter its mouth easily.

When using the Method it is often best to mark your line so that every cast lands in the same area. This creates a build-up of bait and should help your results. Frequent recasting also works to help build a baited spot and attract fish. One final edge that we've seen used to great effect is a long semi-stiff hooklink, a tactic Frank Warwick has used to great advantage. Frank creates the Method ball as normal but leaves a 30cm long coated braid hooklink outside the ball. When the ball dissolves he ends up with a saucer-shaped pile of bait with a lone bright hookbait just off the edge. This tactic has helped Frank bank several bonus fish, including some real specimens.

So don't overlook the Method feeder; it is much underused, but deadly in the right circumstances, and it isn't just for small fish.

HOW TO LOAD A FLAT-BED METHOD FEEDER

To get the best from a flat-bed feeder, you will also need the correct size mould (1). Load the mould with a pinch of method mix, followed by your hookbait (2), then cover with more mix (3). Now firmly push the feeder face-down into the mould (4) to compress the mix. Carefully tease the fully-loaded feeder from the confines of the mould (5). Here is the finished article (6), which will always land this way up on the lakebed.

CHAPTER 14

THE MIGHTY MAGGOT

RIGS FOR WRIGGLERS

Although maggots as a bait is nothing new, it was, until relatively recently, a closely guarded secret as to just how effective they can be for carp, and in truth many anglers just couldn't be bothered to use them. Now things are somewhat different, with a variety of rigs and tactics making them much easier to use. Originally there were two main forms of presenting maggots, the first being the Medusa Rig, which involved gluing maggots onto a cork ball or pop-up to create a buoyant, wriggling hookbait. This technique was very successful but had a variety of pitfalls, including the fact that it was time-consuming to create, and if there were any nuisance fish in your chosen venue you could often reel in a bare cork ball! The second maggot tactic involved tying a small steel ring onto the end of the Hair, then

painstakingly threading anywhere between a dozen to 50 maggots onto a piece of fine line using a small sewing needle. Once you had acquired this necklace effect you took each end and tied it with an overhand knot to create a ball, then tied it to the ring on the Hair. This was, and still is a very good technique and has resulted in the capture of many big carp, and it

is also fairly nuisance fish-proof. On the downside it is very time-consuming and fiddly, although if you use this arrangement it is much easier to set it up with rig wire than with thread or fine line.

Then the modern era of maggot fishing arrived and two presentations just stand out head and shoulders above the rest, the Mag-Aligner and maggot clip, both

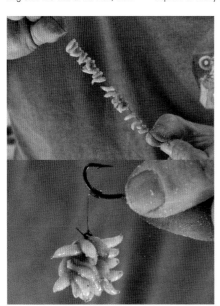

↑ Thread maggots onto a length of light line before tying them to a rig ring positioned on the end of the Hair.

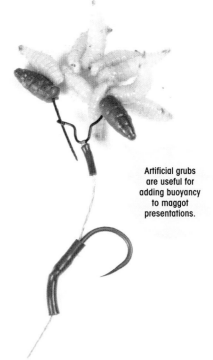

Artificial grubs are useful for adding buoyancy to maggot presentations.

This bag clip arrangement from Solar is the perfect way to attach big PVA bags of maggots onto your rig.

of which have been devastating. The Mag-Aligner is perhaps the simplest to create and use and was invented by Rob Maylin for tackling some tricky southern venues, resulting in huge success on his part. News of his success soon travelled and the presentation is now used by many anglers.

The rig is very simple, utilising a length of coated braid, a Size 10 or 8 hook and a rubber maggot. Strip a short section of hooklink before tying on your hook with your favourite knot. Then thread a baiting needle from the thick end of your maggot starting about 1mm down the side, going just under the skin to exit through the pointed end. Then pull your hooklink back through and sit the hook in place as it appears in the accompanying step-by-step, and that's the basic rig completed.

This hooklink is then mounted Helicopter-style on a lead system, either utilising an in-line lead with a Solar PVA Bag Clip Swivel or a dedicated PVA bag lead. The next stage of the process is to tie a large mesh bag of

maggots that will be mounted onto the bottom of the lead with the hooklink lying down the side. The whole package is completed by nicking two maggots on the hook, then extending the hooklink down the bag before carefully passing the hookpoint through the mesh to hold it in place. This technique works exceptionally well and catches scores of fish.

The next presentation is the maggot clip, which was born to stop the need for threading maggots onto a fine piece of line then tying it in place. A number of manufacturers produce these bespoke clips, which are quick and easy to use. If you simply imagine that the clip is your bait then you can use it in a variety of presentations. The presentation we prefer is a curved shank hook with a maggot clip tied on the Hair, and a small silicone sleeve to trap the Hair in place. The clip is then opened and several maggots are threaded on; even fake maggots can be added to give buoyancy. This can then be fished with a small PVA bag of maggots mounted

> The Mag-Aligna works exceptionally well and catches scores of fish

↑ Two real maggots and one fake one are the perfect hookbait to catch any carp, regardless of the conditions or temperature.

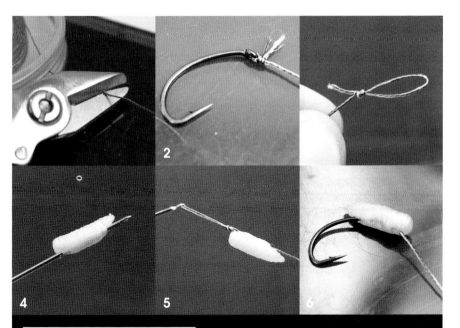

HOW TO SET UP A MAG-ALIGNA RIG

Start by cutting a 30cm length of either uncoated or soft-coated braid (1), then tie on a small curved shank or wide gape hook (2). At the opposite end of the braid, tie a loop like this (3). Next, push a baiting needle through a fake maggot exactly like this (4). Using the loop, pull the hooklink all the way through the maggot (5), then gently tease the hook through the maggot until it sits over the shank, like this (6).

Here's a tip: when using PVA bags, be careful not to burst any maggots, or the juices will melt your PVA prematurely.

straight on the hook or in a very similar style to the Mag-Aligner.

Real and fake maggots are very effective as bait and can be presented in a variety of ways, but these two simple techniques have stood the test of time. It is worth noting that you have to be very careful with your PVA bag of maggots when you nick your hookbait in place, because if you inadvertently nick one of the grubs inside, the resulting liquid will ruin your bag. One final word of warning; large PVA bags of maggots are heavy, therefore strong lines and powerful rods are often needed when casting them over anything other than short ranges.

CHAPTER 15
GOING INCOGNITO
THE ART OF RIG CAMOUFLAGE

We cannot ignore the fact that Korda's *Underwater* DVDs have changed how many anglers now look at their presentations. After watching these films it soon became apparent that our rigs often stand out like a sore thumb while lying on the lakebed. With this in mind, and the idea that 'every little helps' , anglers became more aware of the benefits of camouflaging their rigs.

We have already discussed lines, leaders and tubing but there is no harm in just going over a few facts. Fluorocarbon as a reel

↑ Many modern leader materials have disrupted colour sections to break-up it's outline on the lakebed, concealing it's presence from wary carp.

line is definitely an advantage because it is almost invisible and is heavy, so it sinks. There are other lines that sink well. A good idea if you don't want to go to the expense of spooling-up with fluorocarbon is just to fish a short 10m leader of it, which is both cheap and very effective.

Leaders and tubing help to pin the line near your rig to the lakebed, but the fact that these materials are often thick serves to make them more visible. The first option is to choose a material that

is basically as close to the colour you want. This applies to tubing, leadcore and other products. The basic options are very common; gravel (pale), weed (green), or silt (black), all of which work up to a point. But the fact is that nothing is a uniform colour in nature, so we suggest buying a set of permanent marker pens in a variety of colours which you can use to break up the outline. Thankfully, many manufacturers have already produced materials that have disrupted colour, such as Vardis

> **Nothing is a uniform colour in nature, so we suggest buying a set of permanent marker pens in a variety of colours which you can use to break up the outline**

95

GOING INCOGNITO

With carp in many lakes becoming increasingly rig-shy, it's a good idea to try to match the colour of your lead to the lakebed you are fishing on to avoid arousing suspicion.

THREE WAYS TO CONCEAL YOUR LINE

(1) BACKLEADS are available in two main forms: clip-on or flying. Both types help to pin your reel line to the lakebed, and so hide it from the carp.

(2) TUNGSTEN PUTTY OR SINKERS can be applied or threaded onto the main line to help pin it down. Due to the inconspicuous nature of these products, they are mainly used within a metre or two of the lead.

(3) SOLAR WEED EFFECT is a specialist leader material that is actually disguised as a piece of weed, designed to look as natural as possible in the carp's environment.

1

2

Downfall, Taska iCore, and Fox Submerge. Solar also produce a Weed Effect range which looks just like a strand of weed on the lakebed; this is available in a variety of forms so that it can be used for leaders and hooklinks.

The next really big part of your rig is the lead, and boy, as an example, do these stand out when you drop a dark lead over a sandy area. So, the first basic principle is to choose the right colour for the bottom you are fishing over. With the wide variety of different textures and colours now available it is just so much easier to achieve this. One last point; we have seen loads of different beautifully camouflaged leads that are truly works of art – all finished with a shiny brass loop, and an even more conspicuous swivel! Food for thought, we think.

Your hooklink is the next piece of the jigsaw and obviously the same things apply. Basic colour is the first thing to address, and most companies have brilliant materials that really can blend in. If the lake you are fishing is very clear, why not try a fluorocarbon hooklink? You will also have to pin your hooklink down to keep it as unobtrusive as possible and this can be done in a variety of ways. There are lots of tungsten-impregnated products that can be added to your line or hooklink to sink it, such as those from Fox or Taska. You can also use sinking putty to achieve the same result by creating small blobs the size of mouse droppings and adding them to your hooklink. We also like to use Kryston's Down and Dirty, which is a soft putty that can be rubbed along hooklinks to make them sink.

Hooks and other rig components are also worth taking a look at, simply because so much has changed in recent years. All these types of products have improved so much with anti-glare finishes for hooks being just one example. Take a look at the Gardner Covert range, which has a very subtle green finish. Some anglers still take it to the extreme and use modelling paint to create a camouflage pattern on their hooks. Also, lots of the moulded products, such as lead clips and rubbers, are now produced in some very inconspicuous finishes that really do blend well with the background and cover a variety of options.

97

GOING INCOGNITO

99

CHAPTER 16

SHOCK & SNAG LEADERS

TAKING THE STRAIN

A shockleader is essential when spodding, to take the force of casting a very heavy weight

There is a distinct difference between snag and shockleaders that is often misunderstood, and the definition comes from how we are actually fishing. Shockleaders are used to withstand the force of a cast when using heavy weights; this could apply to anything from distance fishing when a heavy lead is used, spodding, or even using a solid PVA bag. A snag leader, on the other hand, is put in place to withstand any potential abrasion from underwater obstacles that your line may come into contact with, such as gravel bars, boulders, mussel beds, or even tree stumps. So, with that clarified, let's look at each individual method.

SHOCK OR CASTING LEADERS

The ability to cast a long way is governed by many things but predominantly by line thickness, which in turn is affected by breaking strain. As a rough rule of thumb, the thinner the line the lighter the breaking strain. Thick lines do not cast well because they have a high diameter and are often wiry, so using them will limit distance. On the other hand, a supple line of about 0.30mm, or roughly 10lb breaking strain, will cast exceptionally. The trouble is, the 10lb line will not be able to withstand the force of trying to cast a heavy lead to the horizon. If this is attempted with too light a reel line the result will be a crack-off, something that occurs when the speed and inherent weight of your rig causes an overload on the

↑ Whenever you are attempting to cast heavy leads or spods a long way, you should wear some form of protection on your forefinger to prevent the line or leader cutting into your flesh.

built into each end so they can be rovoroed to inoroaoo thcir lifespan. For beginners, this type of line offers good value and takes some of the pain away from learning how to tie leaders. We highly recommend this type of product and have used both Fox Exocet Tapered Mono and Ace Velocity.

When any distance casting is undertaken the stresses and strains placed on all elements of your setup are huge, as is the potential for accidents. With this in mind, you need to be constantly checking your lines and knots for any fault or weakness. Lines also become twisted, which could lead to it wrapping round a rod ring on the cast, resulting in a crack-off. It is a good idea to periodically walk your line out and stretch it, or use a Gardner Spin Doctor to remove this twist. Lastly, always use some sort of protection on your finger for casting. The pressure of the leader on your skin is massive, especially with braid, and the resulting cuts can often be very painful if a glove or fingerstall isn't used.

reel line, which snaps, often in a spectacular fashion. The result of this is that you have to incorporate a shockleader into your setup, which is tied to the end of your reel line using a specialised knot, to absorb the force or shock of the cast. This can be formed from anything like braid, mono or even purpose-designed leaders, and as a rough guide you will need 10lb for every ounce you are casting, so for a 3oz lead you would need a 30lb leader.

There are different types of specialised products that make fishing at long range not only easier but also more efficient. We'll start with lines, because you should look for makes that have a low diameter and are supple, products like Fox Exocet, Kryston's Snyde, Gardner Hydro Flo, or Shimano Tribal. Next we

come to leaders themselves, and several manufacturers have created tapered leaders made from mono. As the name suggests, they are tapered from a thick end to take the strain of the cast, 30lb as an example, down to 12lb at the connection to the reel line. This makes the joining knot smaller, and helps with the smooth passage of line through the rings on the cast.

Now we come to purpose-designed tapered reel lines, which are very specialised but do genuinely make life easier, and also get round the fact that some venues ban leaders. These lines are normally around 200-300m long and have a shockleader

→ Tapered main lines and leaders like these give you added security when going for a big cast.

⬇ Zebra mussels love to cover underwater obstacles and become razor-sharp hazards to the angler.

SNAG OR ABRASION LEADERS

These are put in place to add protection to your reel line in harsh environments, and as carp anglers spread their wings and fish a variety of different venues worldwide, more challenging venues are often discovered, places like Raduta in Romania, Rainbow in France, or the St Lawrence in America to name but a few.

These leaders provide a super-tough section between your reel line and rig. Products like

The famous Rainbow Lake in France, where strong abrasion-resistant tackle is an absolute must.

Kryston's Ton-Up or Quicksilver, Fox's Armadillo, Solar's Unleaded, or Taska's iCore, have all been used by our team to great effect. The thickness and strength of your leader can be adapted to suit the situation that you are fishing. For places like Rainbow where boats are used, you can get away with thick and bulky materials such as 80lb Unleaded or 85lb Ton-Up. In more normal situations where you need to cast, leaders of 45lb can be used to great effect.

Snag leaders don't have to be made solely of braid; many heavy monos can also be used effectively. If you have one in mind, check it out by taking a length and rubbing it over something harsh like a brick. You'll soon be able to assess how many strokes it takes to damage the line and ultimate break. It is worth doing several tests until you find a product that most suits your needs. If your fishing involves casting, bear in mind that the leader knot can be a problem on the cast, particularly with thick mono leaders. Always position a bulky leader knot at the back of the spool prior to the cast to avoid casting accidents.

↓ Dedicated snag leaders come in a variety of makes and breaking strains, and all are designed to overcome snaggy conditions.

SHOCK AND SNAG LEADERS

CHAPTER 17
THE EXPERTS' RIGS
WHAT THEY USE AND WHY

Sit down with a group of 10 carp anglers and ask them what their favourite rig is, and chances are you will get 11 different answers! That's why we've turned to the best, who between them have extensive knowledge and hundreds of years of carp-fishing experience to call upon. Here, nine great anglers highlight their favourite rigs for you to learn from: Terry Hearn, Frank Warwick, Tim Paisley, Terry Dempsey, Rob Nunn, Lewis Read, Nick Burrage, Mark Pitchers, and Ken South. We'd like to thank all these people for their extensive input into this book.

105

TIM PAISLEY
360° RIG

I guess the biggest change that has occurred vis-à-vis my thinking about rigs has come about through fishing two brutal overseas waters, the St. Lawrence River and Rainbow Lake. They both stress the tackle to the limit and can cause an instant rethink on the whole approach to end tackle. The rig I advocated in our two previous Rig Books, published in 2003 and 2006, is a very effective one, but I scrapped it for both the venues mentioned above because it just wasn't robust enough to cope with the demands of those waters. However, recent advances in the development of tackle mean there is a case to be made for what I always looked on as a very successful big-fish rig.

I scrapped the original rig for the St. Lawrence on two counts. One was that the materials I was using weren't robust enough, and the other was that the rig was too fiddly to tie in busy periods during matches. Many of the St. Lawrence swims have a steep drop-off covered in rocks 20-30 yards out, and weed populated with zebra mussels. As a hooklink, Kryston's 25lb breaking strain Super Mantis coped remarkably well with this fierce environment, so when I suddenly discovered that I also had an end tackle problem at Rainbow, it was Super Mantis I switched to there. Again it coped remarkably well, and has continued to do so, although I've recently changed to Kryston's Jackal at Rainbow because

of its colour and the slightly higher breaking strain (30lb).

Both waters are hard on hooks. Part of my end tackle rethink had me switching to the 360 Rig – for which I can claim no credit whatsoever. I switched for two main reasons. The first was that it works, and is a great hooker. Dave Lane designed the rig, and also came up with the design for the 360 hooks. When Dave's involved with anything to do with carp fishing you have to listen, and when you are hooking lumps tight to snags at Rainbow you want a rig that works and a hook that goes in, and stays in. On the St. Lawrence you not only want a good hooker, but when you get in a match-winning situation, or even just a pleasure day of frantic activity, then the fact that you simply have to change the hook, as with the 360 Rig, is a big bonus. One or two of the guys tied up over 300 rigs in advance of the 2011 World Cup! Apart from the chore of having to tie and store all those rigs, they add up to a great deal of hooklink material! In the past, when I have tied up rigs in advance of a session, I've usually changed the setup slightly during the session and then thrown away the surplus tied-up rigs some months later!

My hooklink materials mentioned above for the 360 Rig are semi-stiff coated materials, which I fish at around 9-10ins and don't peel back the coating. I've agonised times many over that aspect, thinking I might be missing a trick, but to my relief I heard no less an authority than Darrell Peck comment at our 2013 Evening of Carp that he

107

↑ Fishing the mighty St. Lawrence River required me to rethink my rig approach to cope with the challenging nature of the venue.

prefers the semi-stiff aspect of an unhinged coated material. To my mind, a hinged coated hooklink is actually easier to eject than an unhinged one. The stiff/supple combi-link works best when the fish sucks the stiff boom of the setup into its mouth. I don't think coated hooklinks are stiff enough to satisfactorily achieve this effect.

In terms of effectiveness in hooking fish, I'm not sure there is much difference between the rig I used to use and the 360 Rig I'm using at present. Both rigs – all rigs – are principles rather than being carved in stone in terms of design. With both rigs I use a sliding ring on the shank for the Hair, partly to add an element of confusion to a fish sampling the hookbait, and partly because my least favourite chore in carp fishing is tying the Hair! Bizarre, I know, but I've

never claimed to be normal.

I've gone through all that thought process because our esteemed Carpworld editor and compiler of this book – Stevie B – has confused me further by assuring me that there are now materials available that will let me use my original rig in the difficult underwater conditions I'm encountering in some of my fishing. I guess I may have to think it out again!

COMPONENTS

- Kryston Super Mantis (25lb) or Jackal (30lb)
- Size 8 ring swivel
- JRC 360 hook
- Micro rig ring
- Silicone rig tube
- 25lb Kryston Silkworm for the Hair

TERRY HEARN

COATED BRAID BOTTOM BAIT RIG

erry Hearn needs no introduction, and his unrivalled success has resulted in the captures of innumerable big fish from a wide variety of UK waters, including seven over the truly awesome 50lb barrier. Here Terry reveals his favourite bottom bait presentation, one which he turns to when fishing over a clean lakebed. Even though the rig is simplicity itself, it is still devastatingly effective and really easy to tie, as you'll see.

Simply strip back 10-12.5cm of the hooklength's coating; I'm using the new E-S-P Tungsten Loaded. Then tie a small Hair loop in the end before attaching the hook via a Knotless Knot. I've tried many different patterns of hooks with this rig, but for whatever

reason, I've always found the beaked pointed type to be the best. In years gone by, the old faithful Continental boilie hooks have worked very well for me, but more recently I've been using a new beaked pointed pattern from E-S-P in a Size 7, which has proved very effective, especially for double 10mm boilies.

When completing the No Knot

it's best to have around three-quarters of an inch of supple braid left above the hook, which will allow it to turn efficiently. Next, slide a 3-4mm length of 0.5mm diameter silicone tubing onto the Hair, which is easiest done using a crochet-type baiting needle, then pass the silicone over the hookpoint and barb, taking care not to pierce the braid

or tubing. Obviously, the length you make the Hair depends on personal preference and the size of the bait being used, but after trapping the Hair with the silicone just past the bend of the hook, almost below the barb, I like to have a gap of around 7-8mm left between the hook and bait. In my experience this is around the right Hair length for this rig when using a 15mm boilie, but if I was using a bigger bait, say a 20mm boilie, then I would use a bigger hook and lengthen the Hair to around a centimetre.

The only thing left to do is to slide a short length of shrink tube over the eye before dunking it in the kettle and then kick it over at an angle, as in the picture. I also add a small piece of rig putty around halfway up

↑ Terry is a big fan of fishing with boilies, and his rig has been designed with a boilie hookbait in mind.

the hooklink, just to make sure it's pinned to the deck.

Once again, the overall length of the hooklink is down to personal preference, but I generally tie them between 15 and 20cm. It's a simple but very effective bottom bait presentation which works best with heavy baits straight from the bag. Here I've shown it with two 10mm boilies, but it's even more effective when using larger baits of around 20mm, or maybe a couple of tiger nuts. Basically, the rig relies on the weight of the bait to turn the hook, and so the heavier the hookbait, the better the rig will work.

As long as the bottom is clean enough, nowadays this is the rig I use for most of my bottom bait fishing, especially if I'm using a lot of bait or baiting tightly around the hookbait. In this situation it's generally better to use a heavy unbalanced hookbait, exactly the same as the freebies. It's a simple, uncomplicated rig which results in great hookholds, and as long as I'm fishing with a heavy hookbait, it's my first choice every time.

COMPONENTS

- New ESP Beak Point Hook
- New ESP Tungsten Loaded
- ESP Rig Shrink
- ESP Silicone Tube 0.5mm

FRANK WARWICK
STINGER CHOD RIG

As I'm sure many of you are aware, the original short rig which eventually metamorphosed into the oh-so-popular Chod Rig was my brainchild. It came about to deal with deep silt on many of the meres, more specifically Redesmere. The rig proved devastating right from the off, and soon found favour with many anglers around the northwest. It was while fishing Manor Farm on the Linear complex that I bumped into Terry Hearn and showed him my version of the Short Rig, which he really liked. The rest, as they say, is history, and he and his mates adapted my idea and came up with what is now known as the Chod Rig.

The popularity of this rig is unbelievable, and it is rare not to see some kind of Choddie cast out on most lakes, whether it is needed or not. Also, with so many different companies providing ready-tied Chods, the presentation is certainly overused on many venues. This, like any type of popular rig, means that the carp get used to a setup and how to deal with it, and its effectiveness falls off drastically. It was with this in mind that I decided to adapt the rig myself; I still wanted the advantages of the cast-anywhere nature of the Chod Rig, but needed it to be more efficient. What I arrived at was a very aggressive alternative to the original version of my short rig.

I came up with this revised version more than 10 years ago,

COMPONENTS

- Longshank hook
- Stiff nylon hooklink
- Shrink tube
- Size 11 ring swivel
- Tungsten rig putty

and have had success with it on a number of waters. It has proved to be particularly effective where the more predictable standard Chod Rig has lost a bit of its effectiveness from overuse. A good indicator to whether the carp are wising up to Chod Rigs is how violent the takes are. If you get a load of bleeps and a bobbin that dances up and down, then you know the fish are still naive about the presentation. If you get a screamer then the fish are wising up to the rig, and the next step will be that they will avoid being hooked by it. The carp can mouth and quickly eject a standard Chod because they can miss the hook slung underneath the bait. This is easy for them to do, which means you can get done time and again without the slightest indication at the rod.

My rig presents the hook above the boilie, which means if the carp is committed to picking up the hookbait it will get hooked every single time. To some it might look strange, and a few of my friends who have seen the rig have commented: "Can't the carp see the hook on top of the boilie?" The reason they can't is because the rig is presented on the lakebed below the carp, so they just see the colour of the bait and investigate. They obviously don't have hands so they explore by sucking things in, and, of course, once they are very close to the hookbait there is a blind spot because the carp have eyes on the side of their heads.

In use it outperforms the standard Chod Rig, and I have had very neat hookholds in the bottom lip with this rig every single time. The carp find it really difficult to deal with, and it seems to have a longer life than the original version. It took me months of messing around with this presentation in order to get the rig to present the hook above the bait correctly because it defies gravity.

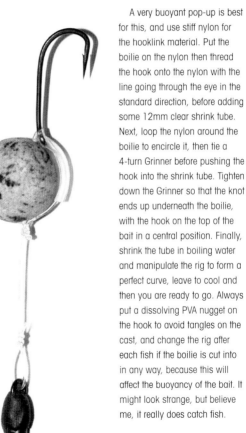

A very buoyant pop-up is best for this, and use stiff nylon for the hooklink material. Put the boilie on the nylon then thread the hook onto the nylon with the line going through the eye in the standard direction, before adding some 12mm clear shrink tube. Next, loop the nylon around the boilie to encircle it, then tie a 4-turn Grinner before pushing the hook into the shrink tube. Tighten down the Grinner so that the knot ends up underneath the boilie, with the hook on the top of the bait in a central position. Finally, shrink the tube in boiling water and manipulate the rig to form a perfect curve, leave to cool and then you are ready to go. Always put a dissolving PVA nugget on the hook to avoid tangles on the cast, and change the rig after each fish if the boilie is cut into in any way, because this will affect the buoyancy of the bait. It might look strange, but believe me, it really does catch fish.

TERRY DEMPSEY

GO ANYWHERE RIG

When it comes to rigs, the most important thing for me is versatility, because I never know what I'm going to face when out on the bank. Think about it; you are wandering round some wild big pit and you finally find some carp head and shouldering at the back of a visible weedbed 70 yards out. I need to react quickly and get a rig out to them, and I don't want to mess around thrashing the water to a foam by casting in and out. Make one cast with the smallest lead possible, feel it down and assess what's down there, and then adjust the rig to suit the situation. If I actually

know the swim I know what's on the lakebed and so can set things accordingly. After all, the last thing you want to be doing is swapping and changing the rigs – it just wastes so much time.

This is the rig I have used in

many different circumstances to great effect, and it's the one I turn to time and again. You do need to think about the situation where you are going to use it, so I have a mental tick list of criteria before even casting out. The main rule is, when using it over a clear bottom such as gravel, clay or fine silt, to keep the eye of the hook very close to the putty, ½ins maximum. This makes it very unobtrusive so it won't potentially spook or put wary fish on edge, but it still retains the great hooking potential of a pop up presentation, which is a personal favourite of mine. However, if you are fishing over thick silt or silkweed, it can be lengthened to around 1½ins; this allows the pop-up to naturally sit over any weed, or not sink into any soft silt.

When it comes to which terminal setup to use it couldn't be easier, as this rig can be used with just about anything; the choice is yours. It can be used with a Helicopter setup, a running lead, or a simple lead clip arrangement. This obviously means that the rig is very versatile and can be used in a wide variety of different situations, and can obviously be fine-tuned to how the fish are feeding at the time. The rig turns aggressively thanks to the fact that it uses a buoyant hookbait, making it an excellent hooking rig, which is of prime importance. Another advantage is that it will always reset perfectly when being blown out or moved by a nuisance fish. This aspect is vitally important to me because I don't want to waste time fishing a tangled rig when the carp eventually enter the swim and want to feed. Hair length is also a crucial factor you need to consider. If the Hair is too long it will wrap around the shank of the hook, so make sure the bait only has enough movement to act naturally and not tangle.

Actually tying the rig is simplicity itself, which is also important. There is definitely no point in wasting your time tying fiddly rigs that often only catch the angler rather than the fish. Just peel off a small piece of coating from a coated hooklink and tie a rig ring onto the end. Then thread the other end of the hooklink through the back of the hook before whipping eight times

around the shank of the hook to form a Knotless Knot. Make sure you keep the Hair very short to stop it wrapping around the shank when you cast out. You should be left with a stiff hooklink and a supple Hair, which I believe is the best for hooking. Thread a sinker onto the middle of the hooklink; this helps it sink and kick away from the lead arrangement correctly. Then tie a loop for the swivel to go on. Just below the hook, peel back a small piece of coating at the distance you want the bait to be off the lakebed; this also creates a hinge and allows the bait to sit at the correct angle. Then tie on a small piece of marker elastic, pulling it very tight, and

then mould the rig putty around it. Tie the boilie on using bait floss and the rig is complete.

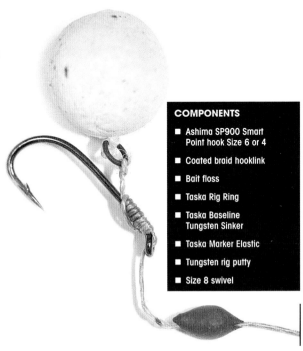

COMPONENTS

- Ashima SP900 Smart Point hook Size 6 or 4
- Coated braid hooklink
- Bait floss
- Taska Rig Ring
- Taska Baseline Tungsten Sinker
- Taska Marker Elastic
- Tungsten rig putty
- Size 8 swivel

MARK PITCHERS

SOLID BAG RIG

Solid bag fishing seems to have fallen out of favour with many anglers of late, and I really have no idea why because it is simply an awesome tactic. Thankfully the guys at Fox know exactly how good it is and have launched some great products to make bag fishing just that little bit easier. Bags are useful in such a wide variety of different situations, and as a carp angler you can't afford not to use them, or at least have them in your armoury.

I use them as a long-range tactic because when tied correctly they cast miles and ensure there is a small parcel of food surrounding the hookbait. They are also the ultimate anti-tangle presentation, because once tied there is no

way that the rig can tangle in any way; this is an aspect that many people forget, yet it is a huge bonus. Up to a point they are also handy – you don't have to worry about what the lakebed is like because everything is enclosed in the bag. This means they are good in weed and over soft or hard bottoms – see what I mean about versatility. They also come in handy when fishing over spodded areas; a personal favourite of mine is to use them when casting to treelines or reeds. You can punch the bag out right to the very edge of the branches or stems and be sure that the hookpoint hasn't got snagged, which can result in the rig not fishing. Instead you get perfect presentation right in the carp's lair. One final edge that I

use in winter is to fill my bag with finely crushed bright boilies; it creates a huge visual dinner plate that can often get that all-important bite when the going is tough. It is a true all-year-round rig and tactic.

With a little practice solid bags are easy to tie, and this is how I prepare mine. Remove the rubber insert from the in-line lead and trim. Slide the In-line Drop Off Kit onto the leader and put the swivel into a trimmed-down rubber insert. The in-line lead can now be attached. Create a small loop in the end of a short length of Reflex Camo and attach a 10mm Pineapple Juice pop-up. I always use pop-ups because once the bag dissolves the buoyant bait forces its way to the top of the pile of bait, which keeps the

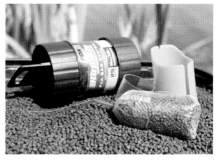

↑ Mark uses a Fox in-line drop-off system to ditch the lead on the take, which can reduce hookpulls.

↑ A Rapide Bag System is used to encapsulate Mark's rig in a PVA bag of pellets before casting out.

rig camouflaged but means it is often the first thing that gets picked up. Tie on a Size 8 Arma Point SSSP hook using a Knotless Knot. Slide a short section of shrink tube down the shank of the hook and a larger section onto the eye. Steam both sections in place, and create an aggressive angle on the section over the eye to improve hooking potential.

Slide two hooklink sinkers onto the Reflex, one at the midway point to pin down the hooklink, and the other just above the shrink tube, to which tungsten putty is attached to counterbalance the pop-up. Slide down a trimmed anti-tangle sleeve onto the hooklink. Tie a small overhand loop at the end of the Reflex hooklink – the hooklink should be around 4ins long, Fox make some great ready-tied bag rigs if you find tying short hooklinks troublesome. Attach the loop onto the Kwick

Change Inline Swivel and slide down the anti-tangle sleeve.

The rig is perfect for PVA bag use because soft supple Reflex braid can easily be folded into small PVA bags, and it will not push the critically-balanced hookbait away from the pile of feed once the PVA has dissolved. The in-line lead is more compact than a lead clip setup, which makes it easier to load into the PVA bag. Also, it has better hooking capabilities because there is nothing to pivot before the fish feels the full weight of the lead. The drop-off aspect greatly improves the safety aspect of the rig, plus it means there isn't a heavy weight bouncing around a few inches above the hook during the fight – something which can result in hookpulls. So there you have it, an effective rig and a great tactic that you should master. It will work anywhere, catch you fish, and even

help you get good presentation where weed or silt is a problem. Go on, get out there and give it a go. I'm sure you will soon become a solid bag addict, just like me.

COMPONENTS

- Fox Size 8 SSSP hook
- Fox Reflex Camo 15lb braid hooklink
- Fox Edges Shrink Tube X Small
- Fox Powergrip Tungsten Rig Putty
- Fox Edges Tungsten Hooklink Sinkers
- Fox Edges Anti-Tangle Sleeve
- Tungsten rig putty
- Size 8 swivel

THE EXPERTS' RIGS

LEWIS READ

HINGED STIFF RIG

I would happily use this rig almost anywhere that I want to use a pop-up and I can get a clean drop on a lead! I wouldn't normally fish a pop-up over a heavily baited particle approach, but over larger items such as boilies, really anything from a single hookbait upwards, it is still my first choice pop-up presentation. Why?

It's tangle-proof and has an utterly unbeatable track record. The orientation of the hookbait and the hookpoint are spot on, and the mounting of the hookbait on the rig ring/D-Rig ensures that when the hookbait is inhaled by a fish it is ruthlessly efficient at nailing it. The loops at either end of the boom allow sufficient free movement for the hookbait to

be taken freely, and the inherent stiffness of the boom works with this to hold the balanced hookbait away from the lead (and potentially the leader). This ensures the hookbait will nearly always settle in a positive position where it can be inhaled freely by any carp browsing on the area.

Take a 12ins length of Trick Link and tie a non-slip Loop

Knot at either end (with one loop incorporating a Size 12 Swivel), so the overall boom is between 15 and 20cm long. If you're not using a Kwik-Lok-style flexi-ring swivel on the Helicopter Rig, you may wish to incorporate a Size 8 swivel on

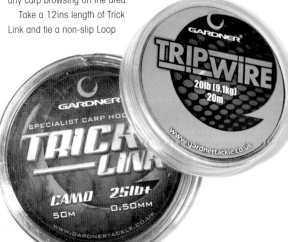

the empty loop at this point.

Tie a length of Trip Wire to the Covert Chod Hook using a Domhoff Knot. Using a tag end up the hook, form a small neat 'D' on the back of the hook with a large Covert Rig Ring, on which to tie/mount the hookbait by threading the rig ring onto the tag end, pushing the end back through the eye, and carefully blobbing the Trip Wire with a lighter.

Make sure the D sits straight on the back of the shank, otherwise the hook will sit at an awkward angle. Tie the Trip Wire hook section to the Size 12 Covert Swivel on the boom section using a 3-turn Blood Knot, and blob the tag end for added security. I prefer to do this before bedding the knot down fully – this way I can manipulate the knot so that the blobbed end sits totally flush against the knot when it is tightened down.

Tie on your pop-up of choice and add the required amount of Critical Mass putty around the top eye of the Size 12 swivel. I normally fish the pop-up between 1½ and 2ins high. I still prefer waxed dental floss because I can use a lighter to warm it, making it virtually transparent. It tightens and melts the wax on the knot, which means very few pop-ups fall off during the cast.

Once this is all tied up, I use a pair of Peel&Pull stripper tools in the loops to hold the boom section under tension while I carefully steam the boom straight to improve presentation and avoid tangles. I then manipulate the Trip Wire hook section so that it has a gentle curve that's in alignment with the hookpoint, and is steady

from the hookeye down to the putty counterweight. If I'm fishing a shorter pop-up, I sometimes fish a slightly exaggerated curve, but I am more confident with a nice steady curve; this doesn't reduce the gape and therefore the hooking potential of the rig – it's a balancing act in this respect.

Attach to Kwik-Lok flexi-ring swivel on the Helicopter Rig using a small section of silicone to keep the hooklink securely in position on the crook of the Kwik-Lok swivel.

Using a Helicopter-style lead arrangement allows you to adjust the height of the top stop (0.5mm silicone and tapered bore safety bead) to allow for different lakebeds. With gravel/hard sand and clay, the stop can be set relatively close to the lead (say 1ins), but where there is light weed, silt or silkweed, the stop can be pushed several inches up to ensure good presentation.

In reality, the key element is the hook section and the hookbait mounting. You can vary the length of the boom and the material used and it will still be a Hinged Stiff Rig – a marvellous and wondrous thing to behold.

COMPONENTS

- Gardner Covert Chod Hook
- Gardner Covert Rig Ring
- Gardner Trip Wire 20lb
- Gardner Size 12 Covert Swivel
- Gardner Trick Link 25lb
- Gardner Critical Mass Putty

ROB NUNN

SAFE BENT HOOK RIG

I t's funny how a couple of poor trips manages to put everything in turmoil and get you doubting your rigs. This happened to me, but it got the old grey matter working; I was thinking about successful rigs that I'd used before, and I remembered the Bent Hook Rig from all those years ago. There was no doubt this presentation was effective but wasn't great for the fish, so the question was if I could create a safe alternative. This is the setup that I started messing about with in autumn 2012, and I started catching very well almost immediately. In essence, it's the well-documented Multi-Rig, but it's been altered from the conventional way of using it to incorporate some rig mechanics that I feel can be key. What this allows, by

using the shrink tube to extend the shank, is the creation of the ultra-successful bent hook-style setup, but in a very safe way, where the shrink tube straightens out when playing a fish.

First of all, the Multi-Rig enables me to use a D-Rig presentation without having to tie

a conventional D-Rig, which can be a bit of a pain to get perfect. Secondly, by threading a length of shrink tube onto the shank and shrinking it at an angle, I can create a safe bent hook effect, which I'm convinced improves the hooking properties of the setup. The piece of shrink tube

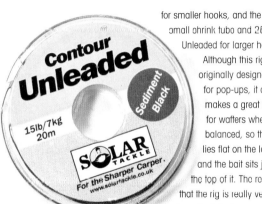

for smaller hooks, and the small shrink tube and 25lb Unleaded for larger hooks.

Although this rig was originally designed for pop-ups, it also makes a great setup for wafters when balanced, so the hook lies flat on the lakebed and the bait sits just over the top of it. The reality is that the rig is really versatile and can be fished over a variety of different lakebed situations. Over clean or hard bottoms I tend to shorten the hooklink down to between 3-6ins, whereas if the bottom is silty or covered in light weed I lengthen the hooklink up to 20ins. This allows the Unleaded to lie over the top of everything, and because it sinks like a brick and is so supple, it really does lie perfectly and the slow-sinking bait comes to rest on top. People may raise an eyebrow at the suggested

length of the hooklink, but don't be afraid to go long. Firstly, it does aid presentation, and secondly, it does no harm to be different. The rig works on a wide range of different terminal arrangements, but I still prefer the simple lead clip setup; not only is it safe, but it's also user-friendly, and works over a range of different lakebed types.

If I'm fishing over a scattering of boilies I go for a traditional pop-up, which I'm convinced the fish can't tell is off the bottom. I like pop-ups because you do get really positive hookholds right in the middle of the bottom lip. Using it with a wafter still gives decent hookholds you can trust, and it also widens the range of baiting situations you can use the rig over. This comes into its own if you want to fish over a spod mix or particles. Talking of particles, this rig works really well with a buoyant tiger nut, whether it's popped up or simply balanced.

119

also neatens up the doubled-over end section of hooklink, keeps the D in the correct position, and prevents it from closing on the cast. Make sure that you leave a small gap between the end of the shrink tube and the top of the D so the small rig ring to which the hookbait is attached has enough free movement to pivot easily.

A small split shot pinched onto the Unleaded hooklink, just enough to sink the hookbait, completes the setup. However, if you prefer to use rig putty, the small overhand knot that creates the looped end section of the hooklink makes the perfect anchor point around which to mould the putty.

I use Solar's Unleaded material for this setup, selecting the 25lb or 15lb material to suit the situation and the size of hook and pop-up. It's incredibly supple, sinks like a brick, and is one of the most robust hooklink materials out there, so pinching the split shot onto it doesn't cause any problems. For best results use the thinnest gauge shrink tube possible; I use Solar's Micro shrink tube and 15lb Unleaded

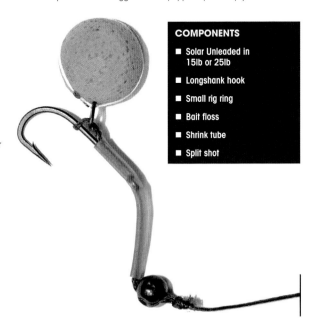

COMPONENTS

- Solar Unleaded in 15lb or 25lb
- Longshank hook
- Small rig ring
- Bait floss
- Shrink tube
- Split shot

KEN SOUTH

INCHODNITO PRESENTATION

KRYSTON®

Incognito

Premium Grade Fluorocarbon

50 mts

18lb   8.2kg

0.41mm Dia

F ishing many waters that insist on a drop-off lead system meant that using a standard Naked Chod was a no-no, so I looked at how to come up with an alternative. Thankfully I managed to invent this in-line drop-off system, so I guess it's problem solved. But there is another problem when fishing the Naked Chod, and that is one of

history. The original Helicopter or Beachcaster Rig was fished on the main line, and this created issues with line snapping due to excessive wear when playing fish. Now I know lines have improved, but I am convinced that the use of shorter hooklengths must put even more pressure on the swivel and the main line.

So to me, the problem is still

a potential flaw within the rig. To be honest, the reason leadcore was used in the construction of Helicopter setups was to minimise breakages caused by the pressure the swivel caused when rubbing up and down the line. Carp fashion is a funny thing, and it's amazing how quickly we forget.

I had to think how to minimise potential breakages caused by this occurrence; in short I needed the effect of leadcore without using it. The answer was simple – take a 4ft length of Kryston 18lb fluorocarbon and attach it to my 16lb main line with a 7-turn Leader Knot. I then slide a Thinking Anglers Oval Bead up the fluorocarbon and place it over the Leader Knot, before threading on a Chod swivel, followed by

another bead. Next I create a Cino loop and coouro thic with a Figure-of-Eight Knot, which I then trim so that it's neat. The TA Oval Bead is pulled down and placed on this knot. This allows the Chod variant to slide between the beads, in effect creating a running Chod.

The next step is to thread on the Shocker Boom, then loop the Size 8 ring swivel onto the end. I then attach the lead drop off style, place a bead over the Figure-of-Eight Knot and fish the Choddie on the line above this. When I hook and play the carp, the Choddie hooklink pushes the

bead down and I am playing the fish on the double section of line, increasing the strength and reducing line damage, and ultimately breakages.

So where and why do I use the InChodNito presentation? Well in fairness, almost everywhere and whenever I can. The simple truth is that the Chod, either in its naked or leadcore version, allows for almost perfect presentation whatever the bottom. Recently I have been using a very short hooklink on the Chod so that my bait is just off the bottom. This is because I am fishing two

waters that have very little weed to contend with, and also I'm fishing over a large spread of boilies, often 2-5 kilos. I think that carp feeding on large areas of spread baits tend to keep their mouths closer to the lakebed. To match the shorter Chod presentation I reduce the distance between the two beads. I have also taken to wrapping the two rubber beads with a thin coating of Heavy Metal. This application pins the beads down, along with the Incognito leader, and as mentioned, the lake's bottom is free of weed, so it helps with camouflage.

COMPONENTS

- Kryston Incognito 18lb Fluorocarbon
- Thinking Anglers Oval Beads
- Size 10 ring swivel
- Thinking Anglers Shocker Boom
- Size 8 ring swivel
- Stiff nylon hooklink
- Thinking Anglers Micro Hookbait Swivel
- In-line lead

NICK BURRAGE

BLOWBACK RIG

When fishing the old Shropshire silty meres, a rig that has served me well is the classic Blowback Rig. So, before I get back down to the lake for my next session, let's have a quick look at my rig setup I like to use for 90% of my angling in the stinky stuff.

I use a supple hooklink because I really like the free movement, and when fishing in all the random depths of silt in Shropshire, it always gives me a great presentation, no matter what the silt depth. I've been using some super-supple braid by Vardis, in the Silty colour, of course; 8-10lns has been working best on these silty meres around Shropshire, but on harder bottoms, such as at Patshull Park's Church

Pool, 5½ins was spot on. The suppleness of the braid helps the rig sit down nicely in any depth silt, whether the lead goes in 2ins or 5ins. There was never anything there to make it stick up like a wrong 'un, just like a stiff link might do on soft lakebeds, and maybe put a carp off from feeding on my little doomed Snowman! (Not to mention the free movement the hookbait gets on a supple braid, when it easily enters the carp's mouth.)

Starting with the Hair for my doomed little Snowman, which is made up of a 15mm bottom bait and a 10mm pop-up, I measure the Hair from the end of the loop to the small ring at 32mm (that's 1¼ins to us old-timers). I use a curved shank hook in a Size

6 which is Knotless Knotted, set so the ring sits opposite the barb of the hook. Then I add 3/8ths of an inch of shrink tube (half on the hook, half off), and once steamed down it follows the shape of the hook. I have found that less is better for the carp on the Mangrove; any more shrink tube or curve and I'm relying on the hook flipping to pierce the lip as it exits the carp's mouth! With less on the hooks, the point is kept free to hook up on the lumps in the bottom of the carp's mouth, as well as it turning as it exits the mouth, which doubles the chances of a hook-up on just the one single pickup! I then just finish with a Figure-of-Eight loop on the end of the hooklink, so I can attach it to a simple clip, and it also gives

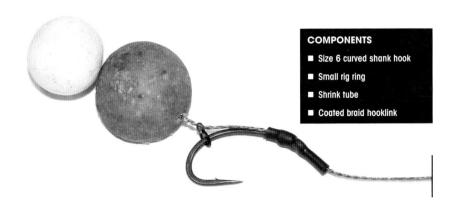

↑ Nick likes to fish his rig in conjunction with a tightly-packed PVA mesh parcel of three boilies. This presentation has caught him loads of big carp.

through the air with no spin at all. The air catches the larger area of the baits, which gives it extra weight to stop tangles (without the extra weight, if you get my drift). When dropping on a tight line through the water, it does exactly the same; with a little help from the foam nuggets it stands off the choddy lakebed (or silt). The PVA mesh bursts open and it sets a little trap of half baits, peppering the spot from slightly above the hidden lead (which has disappeared into the silt), just before the little Snowman takes up its place amongst them. I use it for small traps down the edge and for casting to big baited areas. It seems to put the breaks on the rig in the air and in the water, giving a tangle-free presentation, not to mention whichever direction a carp comes from, there is slack braid for it to easily be able to suck the Snowman into its mouth. (Giving it the shock of its life – and it does too!)

This has caught me loads of carp over the years, and in my book it's simply by far the best. Just try to keep your mindset on course, and know what you are trying to achieve from your rigs.

me the option to thread on bags or stringers. I put a really small bit of putty halfway up the hooklink; this helps it to settle down on the lakebed, and it's job done.

I haven't dropped a fish all year, well apart from the carp that unhooked me in the pads! It happens to the best of us, I'm sure. I found this to be a very good setup that will catch loads of fish. The same hooking arrangement can also be used on a Combi Rig.

It's simple how I set this up so it works for me on the lakebed. I like to use a three-bait stringer set in a triangle; this does the

job and then some! I place three 15mm slightly air-dried Trigga boilies into a stocking-type system and place them in a triangle. I then tie it down as tight as I can, and squeeze two or three of the baits just enough to split them in half, still keeping them in their round form while in the mesh. Thread the hooklink through the centre of the baits, and position the hookpoint between two of the baits; this protects the point and stops the Hair tangling. I finish it off with a foam nugget squeezed on the hooklink underneath it all. This is clipped on to a lead clip, and when cast out it flies

COMPONENTS

- Size 6 curved shank hook
- Small rig ring
- Shrink tube
- Coated braid hooklink

HEAVY   STRONG   TRANSPARENT   THINNER

THE ART OF
DECEPTION

DECEPTIVE™

YOU SEE IT... THEY DON'T!

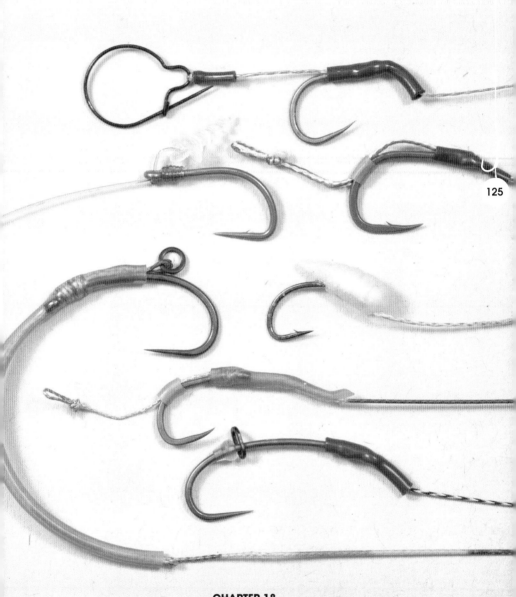

CHAPTER 18

OFF-THE-SHELF
SOLUTIONS
READY-TIED RIGS

Ready-tied rigs have been available for several years but were always considered the poor option. This has now all changed and the quality of this type of terminal arrangement has never been better. The range of specialised rigs that are now available off the shelf is unparalleled, and the build quality and attention to detail has to be seen to be believed.

Rig construction is a time-consuming and fiddly process that many people find tricky; this may be because of poor eyesight, lack of dexterity, or some other type of medical problem. In this case ready-tied rigs are a genuine saviour and help people to get out on the bank with a decent presentation, to catch carp and enjoy fishing. Our sport is now also filled with lots of anglers who are new to this carp-fishing game; they are not necessarily young, just keen to get out and try it. Having access to quality presentations gives them the opportunity to see a rig first-hand and copy it. After all, we don't all have friends who go carp fishing and who we can learn from. Thankfully our tackle shops are packed with a vast array of different rigs that can help everyone to improve and catch. In this chapter we have picked a few of our favourites that we'd be happy to fish with, and which we think are great value.

CHOD RIGS

This presentation is one that loads of anglers find very difficult to tie, the main issue being to actually tie a rig short enough to work effectively. There are loads of versions out there that are excellent, but the one we really like is the one from ACE. It utilises the new Razor Point hooks, which are unbelievably sharp and seem to stay that way for ages. They are also available in short and long versions, which makes them very versatile; it is often short Chod hooklinks that many find super-tricky to tie. We also like the fact that they have a Pop-up Peg mounted on the D, which allows you to change the bait quickly and easily. The last bit is that they are tied using Terry Hearn's preferred Snell Knot, which allows the hook to sit perfectly straight, something that makes the arrangement even more efficient. These hooklinks can either be used as a Naked Chod on the line, or on some form of suitable leader setup – the choice is yours

MAG-ALIGNER

During the colder months maggot fishing really comes into its own, and many waters are dominated by its use through the winter. This isn't to say that it doesn't work all year round, just that it can often become difficult because other unwanted species become highly active as the water temperature rises. The Mag-Aligner is a great rig and has proved to be a devastating way of presenting maggots, but again can be a difficult presentation to tie and get exactly right. This version from Gardner is perfect and makes the job of fishing with our wriggly friends so much easier, and is just one of an extensive range of ready-tied rigs. Based on a coated hooklink, the rubber grub that creates the bent hook effect is positioned perfectly to ensure that the hook turns every single time. If you are an occasional maggot user this will take the pain out of doing it, and will get you off to a flying start.

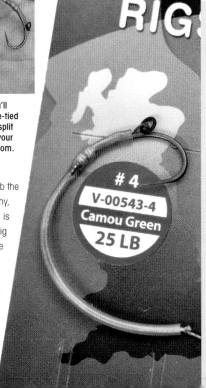

← Simply nick on a couple of live maggots, and Gardner's pre-tied Mag-Aligner is ready to go.

WITHY POOL RIG

This presentation has a fantastic reputation for being a great way of hooking very rig-aware carp, so you would think that it is widely used. The trouble is that it can be a tricky rig to tie and anglers who have poor eyesight or a lack of dexterity, or for those who simply haven't got the time, can often find it frustrating to make. This has now been dealt with thanks to the fact that it is available in a ready-tied version that takes all the pain away and can get you fishing with this super effective rig straight out the packet; in fact, all you have to do is add a shot and a pop-up. Talking of baits, it is important to use a very buoyant bait that will stay like that for however long you need the rig to be in place. This rig relies on the buoyancy of the bait to work correctly and turn and grab the carp's bottom lip. The Withy, as it affectionately known, is a rig that works for carp big and small alike, and is the must-have presentation if you think the fish you are targeting are getting away with it on a regular basis. Try it and you won't be disappointed.

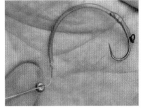

↑ The only adjustment you'll need to make to Vardis' pre-tied Withy Pool Rig is to add a split shot large enough to hold your pop-up in place on the bottom.

→ The version from Fox features silicone tubing to trap the Hair to the shank of the hook, and comes with Hair Extending Boilie Stops so that you can use the rig with either single or double hookbaits of varying sizes.

ANTI-BLOWOUT RIGS

More complex arrangements to fool ultra-wary carp often need more rig components, which can make it costly for the angler. This version of an all-time classic puts a very technical presentation well within the reach of everyone. Vardis' pre-tied rig is put together perfectly and is just one of an extensive range. The rig is formed using a coated braid with 1cm removed below a shrink tube kicker that is mounted on a longshank curved hook, which is famous for its hooking properties. The Hair includes a rig ring level with the hookpoint, which provides movement to the bait and allows the hook to stay longer in the

fish's mouth on ejection because it can slide on the shank. This rig works well with a variety of bait arrangements, but bottom baits or a Snowman presentation is our preference. This rig would be our first choice on any venue that has seen lots of pressure from anglers, and where the fish are noted for being particularly riggy. The above rig from Fox is a very similar presentation and utilises the same principles but is formed using a shank sleeve to trap the Hair and a long kicker/aligner to help turn the hook and grab the bottom lip.

← Vardis' Anti-Blowout Rig is ideally suited to boilie fishing.

CARP RIGS THE MECHANICS

SPECIALISED HOOKS

There are loads of different types of hooks around, but there are few available that take the pain out of tying tricky D-Rigs which aid hooking. This particular model is the Mustad BBS Carp Chodda, which is perfect for a wide variety of pop-up presentations; it not only makes them easy, but also means that you can use a wide variety of different hooklinks. A presentation we've found to work especially well is when it's tied using a coated hooklink. Simply strip about 10cm of coating and then tie it to the Chodda using a Grinner. This should leave about 1-2cm of braid before the coating. This creates the ideal place to add the anchor, whether this is a split

shot, wire, or putty. Now tie the pop-up to the ring provided and you're ready to go, but remember to check that you have enough weight to sink the pop-up. This type of hook also works well with a stiff hooklink material and a wafter hookbait. This is the ideal presentation to fish over areas of clean lakebed, gravel, or sand, and is an easy way of creating a wide range of presentations very easily.

LEADCORE AND SINKING READY-TIED LEADERS

Leadcore and the very latest sinking braid leader materials can be purchased on bulk spools that allow you to make your own leaders, but not every angler has the time or inclination to do this. Thankfully there are loads of companies out there that produce their own ready-made versions which come in two main forms, either a straight leader with a loop spliced in each end, or one that includes some sort of lead setup, like a lead clip or a Helicopter Rig. At first glance these ready-prepared leaders may seem expensive but they do last for ages thanks to the fact that they are so robust. The plain looped leaders can be used in a wide variety of different presentations; all you have to do is set them up with your preferred

lead arrangement. As an example, all you would have to do is thread a tail rubber and lead clip onto the leader. Then simply pass the leader loop through the eye of a swivel, then over the end of it to secure it. Locate the swivel into the barrel of the clip and you are ready to add a hooklink and join the leader to your reel line; we recommend using a Palomar Knot for this. Ready-prepared leaders definitely make life easier so don't be afraid to use them. All the ones we've seen have been well made and are super-strong.

↑ These pre-tied leaders from Taska are supplied with all the components you need to just clip on your rig and lead and start fishing!

↓ Kryston supply leaders you can customise with your own choice of components.

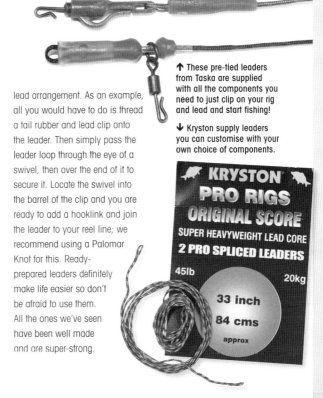